Kyle at 200 m.p.h.

A SIZZLING SEASON

IN THE

Petty/NASCAR

DYNASTY

KYLE
at
200 m.p.h.

FRYE GAILLARD
WITH KYLE PETTY
PHOTOS BY MARK B. SLUDER

ST. MARTIN'S PRESS
NEW YORK

For Adam, Austin, and Montgomery Lee

Photographs © Mark B. Sluder

KYLE AT 200 M.P.H. Copyright © 1993 by Frye Gaillard. All rights reserved.
Printed in the United States of America. No part of this book may be used or
reproduced in any manner whatsoever without written permission except in the
case of brief quotations embodied in critical articles or reviews. For information,
address St. Martin's Press, 175 Fifth Avenue, New York, NY 10010.

Design by Patrice Fodero

Library of Congress Cataloging-in-Publication Data

Gaillard, Frye
    Kyle at 200 m.p.h.: a sizzling season in the Petty/NASCAR dynasty/
Frye Gaillard with Kyle Petty.
       p.   cm.
    ISBN 0-312-09732-8
      1. Petty, Kyle. 2. Automobile racing drivers—United States—
Biography. 3. Stock car racing—United States. I. Petty, Kyle.
II. Title. III. Title: Kyle at Two hundred miles per hour.
GV1032.P465G35 1993
796.7'2'092—dc20
[B]
                                        93-25932
                                            CIP

First Edition: October 1993

10 9 8 7 6 5 4 3 2 1

CONTENTS

Contents

PREFACE

In 1991, I decided to try a book on NASCAR racing. I saw it as the emerging sport of the nineties, and wanted to produce a book not just for the fans, but also for people who are just now making the discovery. I decided to follow one driver through a season, and use that experience as a framework for writing about the sport. The choice of driver was critical, and I began asking a few stock car people for suggestions. I wanted a driver who had a chance to win, but one who knew what it means to struggle. I needed somebody articulate, somebody thoughtful enough to answer real questions, and patient enough to begin with the basics. In every conversation, the answer was the same: Kyle Petty. He is, of course, the son of Richard Petty, the most famous stock car driver ever, and the grandson of Lee Petty, one of the great pioneers in the field. In addition, Kyle is a proven winner on his own, the first third-generation star in American sport that I'm aware of. All of that was appealing enough, but the people who knew Kyle Petty well spoke also of his intelligence and candor, and promised at the least that I wouldn't be bored.

They were right. In the course of a thirty-race season crisscrossing the country, there were flashes of triumph, but many other painful and difficult moments. Through it all, Petty upheld his end of the bargain. He talked openly as the season unfolded, and granted unusual access to intimate discussions of strategy and displays of emotion in a sport that at times is remarkably intense. He invited me to spend time at his home, where he showed me his collection of first-edition books and read poems and stories he had written for his children. During every race, he allowed me to listen as he talked by radio with his crew, knowing that the candor of those conversations might be awkward when he saw them in print.

In addition to that, Petty made himself available for numerous interviews at the track, and in nearly all of those he did his best to talk about his feelings, as well as the objective realities of the race. Nor was he alone. His crew chief, Robin Pemberton, and several members of his crew—most notably his truck driver, Richard Bostic, and engine builders John Wilson and Barry Cook—were more patient and honest than I could have imagined. Petty's wife, Pattie, and his public relations representative, Jane Gossage, also went out of their way to tell the truth, and crew members Jim Sutton, Jim Long, Bob Romano, and Glenn Funderburk answered whatever I asked.

Richard Petty also was patient and cooperative, despite astonishing demands on his time during the final season of his brilliant career; his wife, Lynda, talked with great affection and candor about the intricate relationship between her husband and son. The result, if I have done it justice, is a book that may make them uncomfortable in places, for it reveals the humanity of Kyle Petty and his family and his team—their moments of doubt and anger and fear, but moments also of generosity and class. The latter, in fact, were far more numerous, for the people in racing, as a generalization, are as decent as any that I've met in quite a while. This, then, is a story about the sport. It is not an account of a championship season, though Kyle Petty came close in 1992, and I have tried to capture the excitement of the chase. But this is also a story of struggle and perseverance, which is appropriate for a sport where frustration is a constant, and winning, very often, is merely some phantom that beckons in the distance.

A friend of mine once told me that he likes writing about sports because it's really about life in capital letters. After a year on the tracks, I believe that's true. All the great human stories are there—the courage, compassion, triumph and sacrifice. But Kyle Petty's goal, above all else, is to make sure it's fun. In 1992, he succeeded. I'll always be grateful for that—and I hope that what I've written reflects his success.

—Frye Gaillard

ACKNOWLEDGMENTS

I want to thank and acknowledge the other journalists whose work helped deepen my own understanding. I began with Jerry Bledsoe's *The World's Number One, Flat-Out, All-Time Great Stock Car Racing Book,* which offers a lively and hardheaded look at the sport. I also read Frank Vehorn's informative biographies, *A Farewell to the King* and *The Intimidator,* and Tom Wolfe's profile of Junior Johnson, which first appeared in *Esquire* and set the standard for writing on this subject. Equally powerful was JoAnn Rhetts' profile of J. D. McDuffie, which appeared in the *Charlotte Observer* not long before his death and was the basis for much of what I wrote about McDuffie. In addition, I depended on the daily coverage of racing provided by Tom Higgins in the *Charlotte Observer* and the fine profiles of Bill Elliott and Bobby Allison and the accounts of the death of Clifford Allison, written by Liz Clarke. I must also thank the *Observer*'s Tom Sorensen, Ron Green, David Scott, and Leonard Laye for columns and stories that were useful through the year. I read *The Winston Cup Scene* every week, along with other publications such as *Pit Pass* and *Circle Track,* and often benefitted from the racing coverage in such daily papers as the *News-Journal* in Daytona, *USA Today, The Atlanta Journal-Constitution,* the *Anniston Star,* and the *Birmingham News.* In particular, I relied on Mark Armijo's account in the *Arizona Republic* of the events in Victory Lane in Phoenix.

Most of the material in this book was taken from hours of interviews and observation, and for that I am deeply indebted to the

Acknowledgments

following people, among others: Kyle Petty, Pattie Petty, Lynda Petty, Richard Petty, Robin Pemberton, Richard Bostic, Jane Gossage, Dick Seidenspinner, Kim Long, John Wilson, Felix Sabates, Carolyn Sabates, Dee Jetton, Ansle Hudson, Jim Long, Barry Cook, Steve Knipe, Bob Romano, Jerry Windell, Jim Sutton, Glenn Funderburke, Marty Bodine, John Youk, Mike Ford, Rat Lane, and all the other members of Kyle Petty's team—a good group of people. Thanks also to Chuck Spicer, Kim Mellish, Susie Turnquist, Michael Waltrip, Sharon Petty Farlow, Davey Allison, Geoff Bodine, Dale Jarrett, Ernie Irvan, Dave Marcis, Mark Martin, Alan Kulwicki, Dale Earnhardt, Jimmy Means, Darrell Waltrip, Bill Elliott, Junior Johnson, Dale Inman, and all the other drivers and NASCAR crew members who made themselves available for interviews.

My special thanks, finally, to H. A. "Humpy" Wheeler, president of the Charlotte Motor Speedway, who first urged me to write about racing and who went out of his way to be helpful throughout, and to Mark Sluder and Eddie Gossage, who first suggested Kyle Petty as a subject. I am doubly indebted to Mark, whose photographs and insights enrich this book, and I'm grateful to my friends Karen Garloch, Liz Clarke, and Lisa Munn, and to my stepson, Chris Frederick, and daughters, Rachel and Tracy Gaillard, who read portions of the manuscript along the way. Most of all, I want to thank my agent, Sally McMillan, who believed in the project from the start, and my wife, Nancy Gaillard, who, once again, saw it through. I'm grateful to all.

INTRODUCTION

Kyle Petty was running high in the turns on the 71st lap, pushing 200 miles an hour, as cars often do at the Talladega Superspeedway. It was May 6, 1991, still early in the season, but he was feeling pretty good about the way things were going. He was staying with the leaders as he had all year. In fact, he had led more laps than any other driver, and two months before, he had won the first race at Rockingham North Carolina. He could see a glorious season taking shape—a time when he would step, once and for all, from the shadows of his father, Richard Petty, and his grandfather, Lee, demonstrating some championship style of his own.

All of a sudden, however, his plans were interrupted. Halfway through the second turn, he glanced left at Mark Martin running just below him on the asphalt bank. Petty had great respect for Martin, a talented driver with a car to match his skills, and he was set to battle him two abreast when a third car tried to squeeze between them. It was a reckless move, the kind of abandon that usually came much later in the race, if it came at all. Petty was not surprised when he saw who it was. Damn Ernie Irvan, he thought. In the opinion of many drivers on the Winston Cup circuit, the major league of stock car racing, Irvan was a frightening addition to the ranks—"a hand grenade," one car owner called him. He had been on the tour for nearly five years, and though his talent was undeniable, somehow he still had the judgment of a rookie. He had been blamed already for two or three major wrecks, and as far as the other drivers could tell, he had no grasp of the unwritten laws—

the delicate code of competition and trust among rivals whose lives are in each others' hands.

Now, once again, he was courting disaster.

To the horror of the crowd in the Talladega grandstand, Irvan's car began to inch up the bank—suddenly out of control as it bounced off Petty and into Mark Martin. There was a clash of metal and a scream of tires as Petty spun and Martin's Ford left the track, airborne at 190 m.p.h. In Petty's mind, the next half second was a slow-motion blur. He was spinning in a circle, his driver's door turned toward the cars behind him—seventeen of them, so close now that he could see the faces bearing down upon him. He knew the crash was going to be bad, and he struggled to turn, to point his front wheels back down the track, when he ran out of time and the impact came directly on his door, a sickening crash and a blur of pain as his femur cracked into two jagged pieces, nine inches of it ripping through his flesh.

When he awoke the next morning in his hospital bed, he began to think. Like most other people who are drawn to this sport, who accept its dangers and treacheries of fate, Kyle Petty isn't given to dwelling on regrets. But now those regrets seemed to come in a rush. His ambitions were on hold for who knew how long, and Petty had become an ambitious man. For the past two seasons, in the looming shadow of his thirtieth birthday, he had begun to dream of a championship season—of winning more races than anybody else, or at least scoring more points under NASCAR's complicated formula for naming the top driver in any given year. His grandfather had won the title three times, beginning in 1954, and his father—"the King," as Kyle himself often called him—had won the honor seven times, more than anybody else in the sport. In the seasons leading up to 1990, Kyle had never quite pictured his own name on the list. He raced for the fun of it, and because it was the only life he knew, but he just never figured he would be that good.

Then suddenly in March of 1990, he won the biggest purse in NASCAR history—more than $294,000 for winning one race at the North Carolina Motor Speedway. It was a stunning victory in which he led all but 60 of 492 laps around the 1.017-mile track. He had never driven that well before—had never been provided with a car that dominant—and from that moment on, he saw his career in a different way. There had never been a third-generation champion, but Kyle now grinned and announced to the press: "I really want my name to go on that list with Granddaddy's and Daddy's."

There was, in addition, another ambition that began to take shape, another dream more subtle and grand that he never talked about in public. It was an ambition rooted in the history of his sport—and in his family's storied role in that history. He knew his grandfather had been a pioneer, beginning his career in the 1940s, when the mountain boys came home from the war and some of them souped up their '37 Fords to run a little moonshine back in the hills. In those days, racing was a rough-and-rowdy dirt track sport, run on ovals carved from the clay.

The changes since then have been dramatic. The drivers still possess the same old qualities of nerve and reflex, but those who are now at the top of their field are also spokesmen for major corporations. They are salesmen for Tide or Texaco or Budweiser beer, and the demands today are far more intense than anything ever dreamed of in the dirt track past. So are the rewards. Even a body mechanic on the Winston Cup circuit is apt to make $75,000 a year, and a top driver might get a $1 million bonus to sign, a yearly salary of $500,000 and roughly half of what he earns in prize money.

Fans, meanwhile, turn out every week by the tens of thousands. In 1991, the average attendance for a Winston Cup race—twenty nine of them, in a season that began in February and ran until the fall—was about 115,000.

None of that surprises Kyle Petty. More than most drivers, he's a closet philosopher when it comes to his sport, reflecting often on the levels of its appeal. Most obviously, he says, there's the feeling of power, the adrenaline rush from the speed and the danger that are clear to any fan who has been near the track. But there is also a beauty about stock car racing. From the vantage point of the upper grandstand, or in the glassed-in suites where the corporate sponsors and CEOs gather each week to survey their investments, the terrifying feeling of speed disappears, and in its place is something more aesthetic—a graceful interplay of motion and color. It resembles football in that way—raw and frightening when you see it up close, but with a beauty that increases with a little more distance, a perspective that allows you to see the whole shape.

In addition to all of that, there's the human dimension: the crews who struggle to make the cars run well, like artists mixing paint before the real work begins, or the fans whose devotion is a part of the show. The purists prefer a place in the stands where it is easier to see the whole drama unfold. The greater passion is reserved for the infield, that oval of grass inside every track, where the good ole boys in t-shirts and jeans divide their attention between the cars rushing past and the supple young women who circulate among them, resplendent in their bikini tops, their brown legs glistening in the rays of the sun.

Beyond all this, the most compelling personalities of all are, of course, the men who drive the cars—and none more so than Richard Petty, the King, the last unblemished American hero. It was not just the fact that he won a lot of races—two hundred of them over the course of his career—or more championships than anybody else. It was the way he did it, never straying far from his small-town origins, from the people, the slice of Southern culture that produced him. His house today, in the North Carolina farming community of Level Cross, is less than a mile from where his mother and father once lived in a trailer, and as a mark of his accessibility to the fans, his telephone number is still in the book.

"He never separated himself from the crowd," says Kyle Petty, "or put himself above other people. I think it comes from the way he was raised. There are no pretensions in a small Southern town."

Finally, though, Richard Petty announced in 1991 that he would retire at the end of the following season. The announcement didn't come as any surprise. Petty hadn't won a race since 1984, and his reflexes were visibly beginning to fade. He was wrecking now, with alarming regularity, more than any other driver on the Winston Cup circuit, and even his rivals were beginning to worry. "I think it's time," said three-time champion Darrell Waltrip, when he heard of Petty's decision to retire. "He's historic. He's like a shrine. We don't want anything to happen to him."

Still, it was clear that Petty's departure would leave an empty space, and for the sport of racing there was an irony in that. Nearly everyone agrees that the popularity of NASCAR has not yet peaked, even though the ingredients are mostly in place—the money, certainly, with R.J. Reynolds pouring in $30 million a year, and the top ten *Fortune* 500 companies investing fewer millions in sponsorships and advertising budgets. Television and Hollywood are also interested, and there is talk, now and then, of building new tracks in the country's biggest markets: New York, Chicago or Southern California.

"We're a half billion a year industry right now," says Kyle Petty. "We'll be at a billion by the year 2000." Yet for that to happen, some say racing will need a new star—NASCAR's answer to Michael Jordan—and the need is even greater with the loss of Richard Petty. There are other drivers who might aspire to the role—Dale Earnhardt is one possibility, along with Bill Elliott and Davey Allison—but there is still a void.

Kyle Petty's private dream is to fill it, or at least to play a part—to write his own chapter in the history of the sport in the way that his father and grandfather did. He doesn't like to talk about it much. He understands that he has not earned the right. But with the double-edged burden and gift of his name, it comes to him naturally to think such thoughts. Kyle has a strong and graceful ego, forged, he says, in the fire that comes from being Richard's son.

In many ways, it was not an easy way to grow up. His father was gone a lot from the family home in Level Cross, but the summers were magic. School was out, and the race car families—the Pettys, the Pearsons, the Allisons from Alabama—would play catch or touch football in the speedway infields. "Like a band of gypsies," Kyle recalls, they would pitch camp for a week in Talladega, Daytona, Martinsville, or Charlotte—the kids riding their bikes on the track between races, pedaling furiously up the steep-banked turns, then swooping down at speeds that took your breath.

Kyle was ten or eleven years old before the whole arrangement began to seem "a little odd"—and older than that before he decided to follow in his father's footsteps. His first race came when he was eighteen—a preliminary three hundred-miler the week before the Daytona 500. He had never driven a race car before—at least never in competition—and he could hardly believe the exhilaration when he won.

For the fans and the media, it was "like the Second Coming," but it took him six years to win again. "If ever there was a case of beginner's luck . . . " he says today. The fans were hard on him during the draught, whispering sometimes that he was not a real Petty. But Kyle insists he never felt any doubt. "There's a mentality that has to go with this sport," he explains. "I try not to be cocky, but I never look back. This is the path I chose. Racing is one of those deals where when you least expect it, something bad will happen. It will beat you over the head for fifteen years, but you're always looking at that next race. There's always another week, another race, and every time you think you're gonna win."

That's how it was during the long and bitter months of 1991, when he threw himself into the task of rehabilitation, lifting weights, and waiting for the doctors to declare that he was healed. He was startled to discover how much he missed it—the comraderie and competition, the search for new limits for himself and the car. It was a peculiar life, and a hard one to love, for even the best drivers most often lose.

Still, he knew, with the coming of 1992, that it held the same old magic for him, and when he headed south to Daytona in the first week of February, he was like every other driver in the sport. He was full of hope, working to believe that this could be the year—but knowing, of course, that whatever the lure and possibility of triumph, there was a price in frustration that had to be paid.

PART ONE

HARD TIMES

CHAPTER 1

A BITTERSWEET BEGINNING

The track was dark when the crew arrived. It was Sunday morning at the Daytona Speedway, the grandstand empty, an eerie silhouette against the sky. Campfires smoldered in the vast infield, where the weekend party was now in ruins. Every now and then, there were muffled conversations or the sound of a radio turned down low—a crackle of static and a steel guitar. Beer cans seemed to be everywhere, acres of them, bent and scattered and beginning to smell—a reminder of the way it had been a few hours earlier, the way it always is at Daytona Beach when the crowds pour in in mid-February, parking their campers with the bright rebel flags and the racing banners proclaiming their allegiance. It is one of the oddities of stock car racing that the biggest event of the season is the first. This is not football, where everything moves logically to the Super Bowl. In racing, the first great stop on the tour is Mecca, where they've been racing cars since the turn of the century. Most, at first, were specially built contraptions that looked like rockets. Then the stock cars came in the 1930s, drawn by the legend of the Daytona sands, the hard gray beach where cars went faster than anywhere in the world.

For years they raced on a four-mile course, with long straight-aways running north and south, and short turns through the dunes at either end. The crowds grew steadily in the 1950s, lured by a galaxy of dirt track stars, until finally a driver named Bill France, Sr., decided to build an asphalt track. Already, in 1948, France had been a founder of NASCAR, the National Association of Stock Car Auto Racing, to try to bring order to a fast-growing sport. Now the need as France understood it was to build a facility big enough for the crowds. In Daytona, he chose a spot four miles from the beach, and set out to fashion the fastest stock car track in the country. He built a 2.5-mile oval with steeply banked turns—31 degrees at either end—and a grandstand that stretched for a mile on the straightaway.

When the facility opened in 1959, Lee Petty won the first big race, and in the years since then the list of winners reads like the racing hall of fame: Junior Johnson, Fireball Roberts, Cale Yarbor-ough, Bobby Allison; the list goes on, and no name appears as often as Richard Petty's. As a rookie driver at twenty-one, trying to follow in his father's footsteps, he ran with Lee in the inaugural race, fin-ishing a disappointing 51st. Then he came back to win it five years later—and he repeated the feat a half dozen times.

Now, in 1992, Petty was about to begin his final season, run-ning his last Daytona 500. Everywhere around him the nostalgia was heavy, and some of it, in fact, was officially contrived, as Petty, looking grimmer than most people could recall, was ushered from one photo opportunity to another. He always managed to smile on cue, and to say gracious things about the fans, but he chafed at the feeling of being overscheduled, and the smiles faded quickly when the cameras turned away.

Still, there were moments when the accolades touched him— and none more so than the morning of the race, when Petty and the other drivers gathered for a meeting with NASCAR officials. Such occasions are routine on the Winston Cup circuit, and there is always a certain monotony about them—a quick roll call, a review of the rules, maybe a warning about being too aggressive. This time, however, the routine was interrupted, for at the mention of Richard Petty's name, all the other drivers rose to applaud. Petty nodded in polite response, but the applause continued. Petty nodded again, and the applause grew stronger.

Kyle Petty, sitting nearby, could see the tears in his father's eyes, and soon he could feel the glisten in his own. Part of it was pride, for Kyle had thought a lot about the Richard Petty legend, enough to know that it was rooted in the truth. He had heard the stories, told again and again by the fans—by people like Mel and Virginia Haan, a pair of Floridians, who had explained to a group of reporters that morning how Richard Petty was different from the rest. Somehow, they said, he always had the time for ordinary people, posing for pictures, signing autographs, as if he had nothing else on his mind. Mel had met him first at a little dirt track in Columbia, South Carolina. There was Richard Petty, the King, sitting by himself and eating a sandwich. Haan came up with his Polaroid camera, introduced himself, and asked if Petty would pose with his family. Petty agreed, smiled, then went back to his sandwich. A few minutes later, to Haan's astonishment, the King ambled over and asked nonchalantly, "How'd that picture turn out anyhow?"

"It made you feel kind of special," said Haan. And indeed that was always Richard Petty's gift. He explained to reporters just before Daytona that he had been blessed somehow with an internal clock—an ability to divide his days into segments and to focus completely on the commitment at hand. If, for example, he agreed to a two-hour autograph session, he would always program the clock for three. When that time was up, he would begin to fidget if he couldn't get away. But for the allotted three hours, his attention belonged entirely to the fans.

Kyle Petty knew there was more to the story—a difficult side to his father's personality that was seldom, if ever, reported in the press. Among other things, Richard was a deeply opinionated man, who rarely acknowledged another point of view. In private, he could be overbearing and tactless, lecturing colleagues or members of his family without any obvious regard for their feelings. His rivalries on the track were sometimes nasty—and for a son who was hungry for his father's approval, the King, on occasion, was cool and reserved. But, if those were the qualities the fans rarely saw, Kyle Petty thought it was just as well. If the country was going to choose a sports hero, why not one who saw his fame as a gift— who really believed, after thirty-five years, that it was an honor to be asked to sign an autograph?

So he smiled with pride at his father's acclaim, but he also did his best to keep a distance. In the final analysis, he hadn't come to Florida to honor Richard Petty. His mission instead was to try to win a race.

Every driver has visions of the Daytona winner's circle, of basking for a moment in the flash of the cameras and knowing that his name has gone down with the best. For Kyle, especially, the dream has an edge. The Petty name is legend at the Daytona track, and there is ample motivation that goes with that fact. In 1992, he had something more basic to prove—not to himself, but to those who wondered if his wreck at Talladega would change him, would make him too tentative to be a top driver. Normally, he would have ignored that kind of speculation, for the idea struck him as not worth discussing. In the fall of '91, however, the doubts were voiced by his own crew chief, a plainspoken man by the name of Gary Nelson. "You're just not driving the car," Nelson told him, and Petty was deeply stung by the words. It was true that he hadn't run very well when he came back from his injury for the last few races of the '91 season. His broken leg, though healing, still gave him some pain, and his stamina was far from what it had been. Yet despite all of that, Nelson seemed to be questioning his heart, and it was not the first time.

In May of 1990, shortly before the Coca-Cola 600, Petty was witness to one of racing's tragedies. He was waiting to practice at the Charlotte Motor Speedway, while drivers from NASCAR's Sportsman Division were out on the track. For the most part, these are weekend drivers, many of them relatively inexperienced, who do most of their racing on much shorter tracks—at speeds far slower than 150 m.p.h., which they were running that day at the Charlotte superspeedway. Late in the practice, a young driver named David Gaines was caught in a wreck coming into turn 4. He lost control and hit the wall, spinning to a stop in the middle of the track. Nearly three seconds later, another driver who hadn't seen the caution came through the turn at nearly full throttle. He hit Gaines broadside without slowing down.

Kyle Petty knew it was bad, and he rushed to the scene with his friend and fellow driver, Michael Waltrip. They quickly discovered there was nothing they could do—nothing anybody could do except pray for a miracle of CPR. An eerie silence fell on the track, as soon it was clear that the miracle wouldn't come. Gaines' injuries—especially to his head—were simply too massive.

Petty had several bad races after that—he finished 17th in Charlotte—and Gary Nelson suggested he was thinking too much, was too caught up in the memory of David Gaines. Petty was sure that Nelson was wrong. Not that he hadn't been shaken by the death—obviously, it was horrifying and sad. But those kinds of tragedies were rare, thank God, and when they happened you had to move on. Drivers were like test pilots that way, blessed with a curious certainty inside that bad things happened to somebody else. Obviously, that was true in the case of David Gaines. Petty couldn't think of a Winston Cup driver who wouldn't have been able to avoid that collision. For one thing, they would have seen the caution flag.

So he was stung by the doubts of Gary Nelson, and for more than a year there was tension between them. It never erupted into the open, but at the end of 1991, when Nelson received a nice job offer, everybody knew it was time for him to go.

Nelson did, becoming chief inspector for NASCAR. There was a relief that went with his departure, but Petty knew that for any race team, changing crew chiefs can be an ordeal. It's a position with no real analogy in any other sport—part coach, part team captain—and not even the driver is more important. It's the crew chief's job to make the car go fast—to oversee preparations in the shop, make the calls on strategy during the race, even to help with the changing of tires. The best crew chiefs are gifted leaders, blessed with an ability to motivate and to keep their cool in a high-pressure world. Given those requirements, Kyle Petty knew immediately who he wanted to replace Gary Nelson: his old friend, Robin Pemberton, a sandy-haired New Yorker who was widely regarded as one of the class-act people in the sport of racing.

Pemberton had known the Pettys since 1970. He was thirteen then and working in the family restaurant in the upstate town of Malta, New York, when one day, Richard Petty came in. The King was racing that week at a nearby track, and Robin couldn't believe it when he walked through the door—"bigger than life," he says today. What struck him most was the Richard Petty style—how he grinned and chatted and didn't talk down to a teenaged boy. A decade later, Petty gave him a job, and in 1979 Robin moved south to North Carolina.

That was Kyle Petty's first year as a driver, and he and Robin had a fine time. People called them "the Lollipop Kids"—they were young and brash and laughed too much, but somewhere inside they were also serious. Within five years, they were moving toward the top. Robin was beginning his career as a crew chief, and Kyle was leaving the family operation to become a winning driver for the Wood Brothers' team.

On the surface, their reunion in 1991 would have seemed un-likely. Robin was crew chief for Mark Martin, a quiet, slightly built Arkansas native who had become one of the most successful drivers in the sport. In four years with Robin, he had won five races and fifteen poles, and in 1990 he nearly won the season championship, finishing second behind Dale Earnhardt. But there were also prob-lems on the Martin team—run-ins between Robin and the tem-peramental owner, Jack Roush, including a nasty shoving match in the pits.

Robin had already decided to leave, and he was delighted by the chance to go to work with Kyle—partly because of their long friendship, and partly because Petty, as far as he could tell, was a driver whose career had not yet peaked. Even back in the early days, when he was racing out of his father's shop, struggling most often with second-string cars, Kyle had shown those flashes of promise. He had a 5th-place finish in 1981, his first full year on the Winston Cup Circuit, and the following season he finished 2nd at Dover and 4th at Talladega. With a little luck he could have won either race. His biggest problem was inconsistency, but he was more focused now as he entered his thirties, and he had long since won the re-spect of other drivers. If nothing else, they admired his willingness to go his own way, to forge an identity apart from his father's.

People who knew the Pettys well said he was more like his mother in a lot of ways. He had her compassion, poise, humor and presence; and all of those things, with his teen idol looks—his easy smile and flashing eyes and hair that tumbled in curls toward his shoulders—made him hot property in the stock car world. The sponsors loved him and so did the fans. In Pemberton's opinion, the only thing between Kyle and the top rung of stardom was winning more races—and the season coming up was the season to start.

Those were the feelings they brought to Daytona—a sense of history and a love of the game, and a belief in what the future might hold. "I want to win three or four races and run consistently," Petty told one reporter. "If I said I wanted to win one race and finish in the top 10 for the season, I would be setting a goal that's too easily attainable. I want more than that." He knew when he said it that he was sounding a lot like every other driver, for spirits are high in Daytona Beach. It's easy to hope when the season hasn't started.

Still, for Petty, there was good reason for it. In the practice sessions, he was one of the fastest cars out there, running consistently at 190. The year before, in the Daytona 500, he had been battling for the lead with three laps to go, only to be wrecked by Dale Earnhardt. He thought this car might run even better, and his first opportunity to test that conviction came on Thursday, the day for the first of two qualifying heats. These were short races, 125 miles, and Petty was loose as he waited for the start. He was still in a black, KYLE PETTY t-shirt with the sleeves of his firesuit tied around his waist; he was chatting, smiling, hugging his wife, posing for the television cameras with his father.

When the green flag came, he got off quickly, and within a lap he was running with the leaders. Dale Earnhardt was first, with Dale Jarrett and Sterling Marlin right behind, followed by Petty, Mark Martin, and Terry Labonte. Earnhardt and Martin were no surprise. They were always up there. Labonte was steady—a quiet Texan who let his car do the talking—and Sterling Marlin had been flying all week. Jarrett, however, was a question mark. It's not that he wasn't a capable driver, or hadn't been raised with racing in his blood. His father, Ned Jarrett, was a Hall of Famer, and people said Dale had many of his qualities. He was intelligent, competitive, and unpretentious, but, like a lot of second-generation drivers, he was never too sure, as he told one reporter, "that you inherit the knowledge of how to drive a race car." At thirty-five, he had won one race on the Winston Cup circuit—the previous year at the Michigan Speedway. That, along with his other qualities, was enough to give him credibility with Joe Gibbs, the champion coach of the Washington Redskins.

Gibbs had bought a NASCAR team, picking Jarrett as his driver, and they set about building a team from scratch. Jarrett understood that it wouldn't be easy, but he was eager to get the season off right, and was pushing hard in this first Daytona race. Even when his car began to get loose—a sensation many drivers compare to running 190 m.p.h. on ice—he refused to back off. It worked for a while, but on lap 36, he lost control. His car fishtailed coming out of turn 4, and it happened that Kyle was right behind him.

With a little luck Petty might have been able to escape the collision. He had fallen behind after a bad pit stop, but between laps 30 and 36, he had charged from 16th position to 6th. "Kyle Petty is coming in a hurry," declared Eli Gold, the resonant voice of the Motor Racing Network. Unfortunately, Petty made it back to the front of the pack just in time to get caught in Jarrett's spin—and all of a sudden his race day was over. The #42 Mello Yello Pontiac, dented in places beyond recognition, came gliding to a halt on the infield grass.

Petty climbed out and stalked away. "Not now, man," he snapped, when a TV cameraman tried to intercept him. A few seconds later, he saw Joe Gibbs, staring forlornly at the wreckage of his car—$60,000 worth now in a heap. Petty shook his head and forced a smile. "More expensive than a fumble, isn't it, Coach."

Dale Jarrett was gracious. "I just messed up," he said. "I hate that Kyle got caught in it too."

Ten minutes later, Petty was calm. A reporter told him about Jarrett's comments, and he nodded quietly in appreciation. "I hate it for Dale," he said. "It's not his fault. You try some things in a race like this. He had every right to be where he was."

That kind of interaction is common in racing. The tension can build in the heat of competition, but there is also a pressing need to get along. Racers are like a family in that way, a band of gypsies, moving every week from track to track, preparing for every race in the same garage. "You may get mad," explains Mark Martin. "But you know you're going to see each other next weekend. You have to find a way to work it out."

There are lapses, of course, moments of rage when harsh things are said, and occasional grudges that grow out of that. Kyle Petty remembers the one that simmered for years between his father and Bobby Allison, sometimes spilling into ugly moments on the track. Once in North Wilkesboro, North Carolina, they turned their cars into battering rams, taking aim at each other for four hundred laps. "It was a show of stupidity," says Kyle, "a lot of small-minded jealousy and insecurity." It was also a moment out of character for Richard Petty and Bobby Allison, both of whom believed, and had taught their sons, that when a race was over, you had to let it go. There was always another one just ahead, and too much baggage if you didn't move on.

In February of 1992, Kyle did his best to remember that lesson, but the wreck with Jarrett was still a bitter pill. They had come to Daytona—the most prestigious race in the sport, and one that his father and grandfather had won—with a good chance to win it. Now his car was destroyed, and he knew from testing that his backup car was not very good. He would be starting near the back in the big race Sunday, and though in public he put a brave face on it—"We'll be all right," he'd told one reporter—on Saturday night he confided to a friend: "We'll be lucky if we can even finish."

Sunday morning rolled in cloudy and cold. You never knew about the Daytona weather; sometimes in February it felt like winter, other times it was hot. This particular week had seen some of both, with a damp chill on the morning of the race. When they opened the track, the fog was so thick that you couldn't see from one end of the grandstand to the other. "Not quite the brilliant sunshine," admitted Eli Gold of MRN, but the mood of the crowd was festive anyway. There were at least 140,000 people, and most were prepared to see a bit of history. For one thing, Dale Earnhardt had been running well, and it looked as if he might break his jinx. Despite a brilliant record—fifty-two wins and five championships—Earnhardt had never won the Daytona 500, and at times his luck had been heartbreaking. In 1990, he had a good lead on the final lap, but he cut a tire on a piece of debris, and watched Derrike Cope roar past him for the win. Now, in 1992, he was back. He had already won three preliminary races, and now he set his sights on the big one. "This is it," he said. "We'll be ready."

There was also talk about Bill Elliott, who had one of the fastest cars all week, but everybody knew, as they waited for the race, that the main attraction was Richard Petty. Very few people expected him to win—only those who were thinking with their hearts that he had been in every Daytona 500—a record as remarkable as his seven trips to Victory Lane, and that alone was reason to cheer. Petty was the honorary grand marshal. He waved to the crowd and flashed a grin beneath his cowboy hat and dark sunglasses, and when he gave the command to start the race, he took a few liberties with the usual script. Instead of the ceremonial, "Gentleman, start your engines," delivered with a pomp that never seems to fit, Petty cleared his throat and mumbled: "Okay, guys, crank 'em up."

They were off in a roar so loud it was hard to comprehend. Kyle Petty was starting 33rd in the field of 42, hoping for the best. Within a few laps he was losing ground. Despite the last-minute efforts of his crew—they had gotten to the track that morning before dawn—they still didn't feel very good about the car. The chassis was tight and pushing through the turns, which made it hard for Petty to steer. Sometimes those problems will correct themselves; cars tend to loosen the longer they run. But Petty's got worse, and one by one the other drivers passed him—Terry Labonte, Dale Jarrett, Alan Kulwicki.

"Just hang with it," said Robin Pemberton, and his tone was grim. As the new crew chief, he felt responsible. Maybe they should have done more testing on the backup car. Maybe they should have tried a different chassis setup, different springs or a different set of shocks. There was no use worrying about it now. All he could do was offer encouraging words on the radio, and wait for a chance to make a pit stop. Despite these hopes, the laps ticked away without a caution flag, and Petty dropped back all the way to 41st. It was astonishing, really—here he was next to last in a race that he had once believed he could win. Still, he knew it was no time to panic. They hadn't even reached the halfway point, and there was plenty of time for better luck to intervene. And suddenly, it did—first in the form of a brief rain shower that caused a caution on lap 82, and gave them a chance to work on the car. They put on new tires, and made a few quick adjustments in the chassis.

In about twenty-five seconds, they were back on the track, and Petty reported the car was running better. They were still way back, but moving now at a respectable pace, when there was a multi-car crash on turn 2. Steve Knipe saw it first—a spinning, screaming tangle of cars, colliding at speeds of 190. Knipe is the spotter for the Kyle Petty team; his job is to watch the race from a tower and guide his driver through the trouble spots. Knipe is good at it—a tall, quiet man, not given to panic, but there was an edge to his voice as he told Kyle Petty: "Back way down! Stay low! Stay low!" Petty did as he was told, slowing the car and swerving toward the bottom of the steep-banked turn, and he managed to thread his way through the wreckage.

Later, he would learn exactly what had happened. Sterling Marlin and Bill Elliott were leading the race, with Ernie Irvan running just behind them. Coming out of turn 2, Irvan decided to try for the lead. He dove down quickly to the bottom of the track, three abreast with Marlin in the middle. Elliott and Irvan began to fishtail, both cars caught in a swirl of air, and Sterling Marlin was pinched off between them. Suddenly, there were racecars spinning everywhere—more than a dozen before it was over—and Ernie Irvan, once again, was the villain. It was a familiar role, dating back to 1990 at Darlington, South Carolina, when he was racing side by side with Kenny Schrader. Their cars collided, as Irvan slid up the track, and in the wreck that followed, veteran Neil Bonnett was injured so badly that it ended his career. The fury at Irvan was not so much that he made a mistake; those things happen in racing, and sometimes, inevitably, people are hurt. It was the circumstances that were so absurd. In the wreck at Darlington, Irvan was thirteen *laps* behind Schrader, who was leading the race, and there was simply no need to try to outrun him. The following year, in the life-threatening accident that injured Kyle Petty, Irvan attempted a three-abreast move that was almost certain to end in disaster—and the race at the time was not even half over. That summer he apologized to his colleagues, stood before them at the Daytona Speedway and promised to work harder to earn their respect. Many of the drivers, including Kyle Petty, had to give him some credit for that. Ernie, after all, seemed to be a nice guy, a stocky Californian with dark hair and heavy-lidded eyes, who clearly had the gift for driving a car. As Robin Pemberton once told a reporter, "He's the kind of guy you want to like. He just does some stupid things."

Now in Daytona, he was at it again, making a daredevil bid for the lead when patience would clearly have been a better course. Later, Kyle Petty would feel sorry for him, but for now he had other things on his mind. As he made his way carefully through the litter of cars, he could see that the fastest were crippled or destroyed. Sterling Marlin was out; Elliott and Earnhardt were badly damaged. Petty knew his own chances had improved—and the irony was that he probably would have been in the middle of the mess if his fastest car hadn't wrecked with Dale Jarrett's.

It was such a peculiar sport they had chosen, so fickle and unpredictable at times. But for the moment at least, he wasn't complaining. His backup car was finally running better, thanks to the effective work of his crew, and with many of the best cars out of the way he thought he had a chance for a top 20 finish—maybe better, if he played it just right. They decided to pit during the caution for the wreck, putting on new tires and doing some more fine-tuning of the chassis. When the race resumed on lap 99, Petty was flying. He passed Greg Sacks and Derrike Cope, and soon he was catching Terry Labonte. His laps were now a full second faster than they had been at the start—47.5 seconds, exactly as fast as the leader, Davey Allison. Within thirty-five laps he had moved up all the way to 9th place.

By lap 160, he made it by Labonte, and was now in a battle with Dale Earnhardt. It took twenty-three laps to get around him for good, both cars weaving in and out of slower traffic, but after a three-abreast move coming into turn 3, Petty was 7th and hoping for more. Ten laps later, Michael Waltrip blew an engine racing for the lead, and Petty held on to finish 6th. There were smiles from the crew as he coasted to a stop. It had been a good race, considering the dismal way it began. But as soon as Petty climbed out of the car, it was quickly apparent that something was wrong. He took a few steps, then wobbled and sank to the ground. He sat for a moment with his head on his knees, then slowly fell back and lay on the ground. A team of medics rushed to the spot. They gave him oxygen and put him on a stretcher, and carried him away to the first-aid room.

A few minutes later, he emerged. "I'm hungry," he said. His face was pale, and his long, curly hair was dripping with sweat, but he said he was fine. For the last few laps, there had been some kind of leak, and his car had filled up with carbon monoxide. All it took was a little bit of oxygen, and he was able to smile and face the reporters. He praised his crew and said gracious things about the other drivers, and then went away to be with his family.

The mood was different a short distance away where Davey Allison was surrounded by the cameras. Davey is a contemporary of Kyle's, nearly a year younger but so far in his career he had been more successful. He'd won thirteen races coming into the season, compared to Kyle's four—and it was a comparison, in fact, that a lot of people made. Davey was easily the most successful of the current crop of sons who had followed their fathers to a career on the tracks. Dale Jarrett had won one race. Sterling Marlin was still looking for his first. Davey had been a winner almost from the start, and now he had just claimed the biggest race of all. He spoke with emotion about the race in 1988, when he had finished second to his father, the great Bobby Allison. "Winning this race has been a goal of mine since I watched my dad do it," he said. "This is the best win I ever had."

Meanwhile, for Dale Earnhardt, it was another disappointing day in Daytona. In 1990, he had cut a tire on the final lap. In '91, he had been in a wreck with three laps to go. His troubles this time had come much earlier, and if the wreck with Irvan had not put him out, it had robbed him at least of his competitive edge. He felt lucky in a way to even finish 9th.

Just before the race, Robin Pemberton had told a reporter there are "no higher highs and no lower lows than you find in this sport." Allison and Earnhardt both proved the point. For Petty, however, it was more bittersweet. The season had started somewhere in the middle.

CHAPTER 2

BATTLING WITH "THE DUKE"

The day dawned clear and cold in Rockingham, and Kyle Petty was nervous—more nervous, really, than most people could remember. The second race of the season was approaching, and the pressure was intense; Rockingham had become his track. He had won the first race of 1990, the richest purse in NASCAR history, and he won again in '91. In addition, he'd won three of the last four poles, setting new track records for speed. Now in 1992, the media people seemed to be everywhere, asking their questions again and again. What was his secret at the Rockingham track, and did he believe he could keep on winning?

One crew from a television station even approached him as he tried to slip away and go to the bathroom. "Come on in, guys," he snapped. "Let's get the whole thing down on tape."

Petty had his reasons for being tight. For one thing, with

a new crew chief it was important for the team to get off right, and already there were a number of outside distractions. Reporters kept asking about Robin Pemberton, wondering if he could fill Gary Nelson's shoes. Petty considered the question absurd. It was true that Nelson had more experience, but if you looked at their records for the last four years, Robin's was better. His cars had won five races to Nelson's two, fifteen poles to Nelson's four. Petty, however, knew that Robin was feeling the pressure, partly because he was so conscientious. He was the kind of man who drove himself hard, expecting perfection or something close to it, while he tried to go easy on the feelings of his crew. Petty appreciated that about him. There was nothing more delicate than building a good team. The work was hard, the hours were long, and a driver was only as good as his car. Kyle had learned that much in the early days with his father, when he did a little of everything around the shop—welding, sanding, putting on shocks. He even put in some time in the pits. Once in a race in California, he was substituting as jack man for the King. He had never done it before, but the job on its face seemed easy enough: just jack up the car when it was time to change tires. He was young and cocky, slinging the jack on the first pit stop, when he slammed it accidentally into the side of the car. His mistake left a dent, and threw off the timing on the change of tires "Get a new jack man," growled Richard Petty. "This one can't hack it."

Years later, Kyle Petty would laugh as he told the story—a commentary on the foolishness of youth. At the time, however, it wasn't funny, and he vowed as a driver—particularly as he grew more reflective about it—that he would never criticize the mistakes of his crew. "And he doesn't," says Richard Bostic, who drives the truck that hauls Petty's cars. "He can be hard on himself, but almost never on anybody else. You just won't find a driver more considerate, or easier to work with."

The result has been a team of high morale, and Kyle knew Robin would fit in well. But the reporters were out there asking their questions, and though Robin, on the surface, was uneffected by it—he was laughing and telling jokes as they worked on the car—Petty recognized the early symptoms of pressure. He wanted to do well for the sake of his friend, but the task this time was daunting at best. Nobody had ever won three straight poles at Rockingham, and as they practiced Friday morning before qualifying, Petty's was not the fastest car on the track. Bill Elliott's and Mark Martin's were both a little quicker, and there were two or three others that were right in there. But Petty had confidence in his Rockingham car, even a certain affection for it. They had named it The Duke, after John Wayne, and for several years now it had blown away the competition. The problem was, Gary Nelson had built it. He knew its secrets, every little place where it skirted the rules, or pushed at the edges, and Nelson was now the chief inspector for NASCAR. "Don't even bring it to the track," he had warned them. But Petty and his team just couldn't resist. They swapped serial numbers with another car, and changed the name plates they glued on the dash: It was now Rhett Butler instead of The Duke.

For the next several days, they let it slip in conversations around the track that they had decided reluctantly to try a new car. It was risky, they said, but The Duke was getting old, and Robin, after all, had to make his own mark. They could only imagine what would happen if Gary Nelson caught them. He had been aggressive in his duties as chief inspector, and while many people in the sport had praise for his integrity, a piece of grafitti had appeared in Daytona, big block letters in the drivers' bathroom: GARY NELSON IS A DICKHEAD.

He had certainly been tough on Kyle Petty's team, giving them trouble during inspections in Florida. They expected more of the same in Rockingham, but amazingly enough, their subterfuge worked. The Duke in disguise sailed through without a hitch, and when qualifying began on Friday afternoon, the question was not whether Petty was fast, but whether the other teams had caught up.

Derrike Cope went first, and he was not a problem. His best of two laps was less than 145 m.p.h.—nowhere close to Kyle Petty's record. Chad Little went next, and he was even slower. Still, Petty's nerves grew worse the longer he waited, and even his prayers seemed to give him little comfort. His grandfather had come by a few minutes earlier, making a rare appearance at the track. The old man quit the sport cold turkey in the 1960s, indulging a newfound passion for golf. Kyle was grateful that he came this day, grateful for the pride that he saw in his eyes. Yet in another way, it only added to the pressure. What if he let the old man down?

When his turn finally came, after a pretty good run by Kenny Schrader, he knew he had to banish the distractions from his mind—just concentrate on driving the car, pushing it as hard as he could in the turns, almost to the point where he thought it would spin. He took a deep breath and stood on the gas: His first lap was quick, he knew that much, and the second time around seemed to be even faster. But the car was so smooth, it made him worry. Maybe, somehow, he hadn't pushed it to the edge. When he rolled to a stop, he was still unsure, but the crowd was cheering and people from his team were rushing toward the car. He had set a new track record, they said, 149.926.

Petty felt a rush of gratitude and relief, but he also knew this was no time to celebrate. Twenty-three drivers still had to qualify, and included in the group were Elliott and Martin. He needed a place to hide out from the press, at least until he knew if he had won, and he decided to head for Richard Petty's trailer. The King hadn't qualified well that day, and by Kyle's account that's what they discussed. "We talked about his car," he said. "We didn't talk that much about mine."

Strange as it sounds, that's probably true, for Kyle has developed a reserve around his father, a reluctance to take great risk with his feelings. There have been some awkward moments through the years. Kyle's wife, Pattie, remembers the Christmas when Kyle gave his father a motorcycle and was clearly stung by the lack of response. "I know what he wanted," Pattie said months later. "He wanted his dad to reach over and hug him. But I'm not sure Richard even knew how. . . . I have never seen his daddy put his arm around him and say, 'I love you.' Kyle's daddy grew up in a different time."

If Kyle has been hurt by his father's reserve, it is nevertheless true that he admires Richard Petty. "You always compete with your father," he says, "trying to throw a football better or whatever. But it was always him that taught you how to throw it." As the years went by, he came to believe there was no better teacher than the King—especially when it came to the art of racing cars. So he made his way to his father's truck, chatting idly for awhile in that haven, until finally word reached him that he had won. He had beaten Bill Elliott by a tenth of a second and Mark Martin by two-tenths. For the third straight time, he was on the pole.

It's a feat with no analogy in any other sport. Ostensibly, the point of the qualifying laps is to determine the starting order of the race. In actuality, the stakes are higher than winning the toss in a football game, or being seeded first in a tennis tournament. In the minds of most drivers, pole day is a test. They are out there alone for a couple of laps, nothing to distract the attention of the crowd. The embarrassment stings if they don't do well, but if they win it's a part of their record—and a welcome contribution to the morale of the team.

In Rockingham, the people on Petty's team were ecstatic, particularly the owner, Felix Sabates. He found Jim Long, who had made the final adjustment on the car—a minor change in the pressure of the tires—and by way of thanks, Felix gave him a watch: a Rolex worth about $10,000. The gesture was not out of character for Sabates, a millionaire businessman from Charlotte who left his native Cuba to get away from Castro. The Sabates family had opposed the revolution, and one by one they slipped away to the north. The day Felix left, June 9, 1959, he was alone, a good-looking boy not quite seventeen. He was armed with twenty-five dollars in his pocket, a couple of boxes of Cuban cigars, and a piece of wisdom from his grandfather, José.

"If things get bad," the old man said, "and you have nothing to eat, get a toothpick and put it in your mouth. That way, people won't think you are hungry and that you are a bum. You won't lose your dignity."

That moxie has defined Sabates ever since—from the hard, early years of menial jobs, through the time of selling cars in a Charlotte dealership. By the 1970s, he had his own company, which imported and sold electronics. His big break came when a firm called Atari asked him to market a strange new game. They called it "Pong"— Ping-Pong played on a video screen—and it launched a craze that soon swept the country. From there, Sabates moved on to other toys, including Nintendo. Before long he was rich, with annual sales of $400 million.

In 1988, he bought a race team, and with Kyle as his driver, he soon emerged as a popular figure in NASCAR—a man of generosity and charm who quickly made friends at every level of the sport. It was true that he had a considerable ego, and when his temper went off it was something to see. "The Cuban Tornado," one team member called him. But there was no sign of that at the Rockingham track when his team won the pole, and he laughed and told jokes and took the whole crew for a dinner of steaks.

Throughout the festivities, Kyle Petty did his best to keep an even keel. He was committed, as always, to having a good time, and he had to admit it was easier when you won. But he had also learned in the days with his father that fortunes can change very quickly at the track. He remembered the time in 1976 when the King and David Pearson were racing side by side in Daytona. On the last lap they collided, and Richard's car spun—coming to a stop 100 yards from the finish.

"His car wouldn't crank, so all of us ran out to push him across," says Kyle, who was fifteen at the time and watching with the rest of the family from the pit. "It was completely illegal, and Pearson beat us to the finish anyway. So Daddy gets out as calm as could be and he says, 'Okay, guys, this race is over. It's time to start getting ready for the next one.' "

The King was the same on the good days too. He enjoyed the moment, and then let it go—and within twenty-four hours after winning the pole, Kyle was beginning to do the same thing. He had made his rounds among the reporters, praising Robin and the members of his crew, particularly Jim Long and the engine builder, John Wilson. On Saturday, he retreated, finding a little time for himself, as he sank back quietly into a couch in his trailer. "For the past two or three years," he said, "Rockingham has been like a haven to us. Something about this track has really clicked. You can't define it. You just try to enjoy it. It'll probably go away just like it came."

Petty smiled and closed his eyes. For the moment at least, he was pleased. The season was beginning to take shape as it should.

The morning of the race was breezy and warm. The March winds were fickle, and there was not a cloud in the steel blue sky. Robin

Pemberton felt funny as he waited, worried about the car. It had performed superbly in qualifying, but to Robin the setup didn't make any sense. The springs, the shocks, the motor, the weights—everything seemed wrong. Still, Robin was new, and this was The Duke, the terror and the scourge of the Rockingham track, so he held his tongue and suppressed his doubts, and let himself get caught in the mood of the day.

"The story of this race is Kyle Petty," boomed Eli Gold of MRN, and that seemed to be the opinion everywhere. Driver Ricky Rudd told one reporter that his car was running well, and he only hoped at some point that he could "see the back bumper" of the Mello Yello Pontiac. For his part, Kyle seemed cool and relaxed as the crowd poured in through the Carolina pines, parking their cars in the groves of trees and trudging up the last steep hill to the stands. The track had a long and dramatic history, dating back to the 1960s. Richard Petty had won eleven races there, Cale Yarborough seven and David Pearson five. Now Kyle's own name was a part of the lore, and he would soon have a chance to add another chapter.

He knew, however, that it was dangerous to take anything for granted. Bill Elliott was starting on the front row beside him, and Petty thought it was important to get off well. He wanted to make sure he led some laps early. For one thing, he would get five points for leading a lap, and every little bit helped in the championship race. More than that, he wanted to find his own pace at the front where it was sometimes easier to stay out of trouble.

They started fast with Elliott and Petty side by side. Within a lap, Petty had the lead, though Elliott was still pushing hard on his bumper. Within two laps, the lead was getting bigger, and Robin's voice on the radio was calm: "You're doing it, man. Settle down, run your own race." The lead kept growing for the next several laps, reaching ten car lengths as they started the sixth. "Sayonara," said a voice in the press box.

On the track, however, something funny was happening. Kyle had run the fifth lap in 25.30 seconds—nearly a full second slower than his qualifying time. The next time around, it was 25.60, and by lap 8 it was 26-flat—every lap a little slower than the last.

Bill Elliott was gaining on him now, and on lap 11 he ducked low to pass.

"We are a little bit loose," Petty told his pit, but his radio voice was clinical and calm. This was no time to panic, even with Elliott soon stretching his lead and Kyle's lap times getting steadily worse: 26.10, 26.40, 26.60. The bad news came on lap 18. Petty reported the car was "pushing" through the turns, while at other times it was still running loose. A race car usually does one or the other. Either the front end pushes because it's adjusted too tight, making the steering stiff and unresponsive, or the car tends to spin because the rear is too loose. Almost necessarily, the solution for one problem makes the other one worse.

Robin suddenly felt a little sick—angry at himself for not listening to his doubts. Kyle was now barely holding on to second, with Brett Bodine and Rusty Wallace closing fast, and Mark Martin only a car length behind. But on lap 23, they got a reprieve. Veteran Dave Marcis blew an engine, which caused a caution and gave the crew some time to work on the car. The question was, what to do. Should they loosen the chassis to keep it from pushing, or might that make it even harder to handle? There didn't seem to be a good answer, so Petty suggested they try to live with it. They decided to put on four new tires, hoping that would at least mask the problem. Unfortunately, they also got a bad pit stop—23.9 seconds, at least four seconds slower than they would have liked—and Kyle was running fourth when the race restarted. Amazingly enough, he was also fast and within three laps he had moved back to first.

He ran that way for thirteen laps, moving past Elliott and Rusty Wallace, but in his mirror he could see there was trouble on the way. Davey Allison had started the race 10th, and he had been moving steadily through the traffic all day. By lap 42, he was bearing down on the leaders, passing Rusty Wallace and taking aim on Kyle. On lap 43, Davey took the lead, as Petty once more began to struggle. His four new tires were beginning to wear, and the car wasn't handling as well in the turns. For awhile, the problems didn't seem overwhelming, and he held on to 2nd for the next seven laps. But his fade grew worse as he fell to 5th by lap 66, and all the way to 8th by lap 85. Every time there was a caution, they worked on the car, trying desperately to find the right adjustment. They battled back to 5th by lap 140, but faded again as the car got loose.

"It's bad now," Petty told the pit, and his voice was resigned, almost despondent. The battle continued for nearly three hundred laps, and after a while they knew they had lost. The Duke ran well in a burst here and there, just as it had when Petty won the pole. But the longer they ran, the worse it got, and with sixty-five laps to go in the race, it quit altogether. They discovered a crack in the camshaft—a part that is made out of solid steel and ought to be impervious to that sort of thing.

"Just one of them days," Petty told the reporters, the same ones who had wondered a few hours earlier if his car was invincible in Rockingham. Their questions now had a tone of disbelief. How had he managed to run so badly? Petty was patient as he tried to give an answer: The car was pushing sometimes, loose at others— it was just a bad day. As their questions continued, he began to smile. He got a kick out of writers sometimes. They always managed to sound so grave, like they were writing about the fall of the Berlin Wall. It was just a race, he finally told them, and another one would start in less than a week.

A few feet away, Robin forced a smile, and ran his fingers through his sandy-blond hair. He was already brooding about The Duke. They had gone to such trouble to bring it to the track— changing the name plate, and telling Gary Nelson and the rest of the world that it was really a new car they had named Rhett Butler. After all that, the damn thing betrayed them. But it was only a car, and there was no need to get superstitious about it. With a few adjustments it ought to be okay.

Robin thought about it overnight, and as much out of stubbornness as anything else, he decided to take it the next week to Richmond.

Richmond is a place that holds mixed memories. Kyle Petty won his first race there—a bump and grind finish in 1986. With three laps to go, Dale Earnhardt was leading the race, when Darrell Waltrip passed him. Earnhardt tried to pass him back, but clipped a fender and both cars spun. Petty was 5th, a safe distance back, and he could see the smoke from the melee of cars. He was startled to discover, when he came to the spot, that the wreck had engulfed not only Earnhardt and Waltrip, but the 3rd-place car of Geoff Bodine and 4th-place Joe Ruttman. There was nothing ahead but open track, and Petty cruised home to win by default. After the race he said it was luck—probably caused by the new underwear he had bought that morning. People thought he was joking, but he wore the same pair for the rest of the season (and finished 10th in the championship race).

Except for that, nearly all of his luck in Richmond was bad. He did finish 6th in 1990, but it was the only other time he even came close.

In 1992, however, things looked better. The Duke was so fast on the first day of practice that Petty called home and told his wife, "Man, we're flying." His qualifying run confirmed that assessment. There were several fast cars that had started before him—particularly Alan Kulwicki, who qualified at 120.125 on a track that was barely three-quarters of a mile. But a few cars later, Petty beat him by seven hundredths of a second, and once again he held his breath. Would that be good enough for the pole?

Although the time held up for twenty-seven cars, in the end Davey Allison was quicker, and Bill Elliott beat them both by a tenth of a second. Nevertheless, the disappointment came and went in a flash. Starting third would put Petty on the second row inside, and at this particular track the low groove was the best. If the car ran well—and they had worked on it hard since the Rockingham disaster—he would be in good shape.

The next morning, it rained—a cold, ugly day, which was not unusual for Richmond in March. When they finally got to practice, they were appalled: The Duke was one of the slowest cars on the track. It was okay in sprints, as it had been the day before when they qualified, but when they set it up to run for four hundred laps, nothing about it seemed to work right at all. As far as they could tell, the biggest problem was the gear ratio—which meant the engine was too strong for the car. The wheels were spinning coming out of the turns, and sometimes all the way around the track. It was not an easy problem to fix: they needed time for trial and error. With their practice shortened by the cold March rains, all they could do was make an educated guess.

They retreated to the office on the transporter truck, and began to hash it out. There was a certain desperation in the air, and after a while, Dick Seidenspinner decided that he had seen enough. Seidenspinner is the business manager of the team—a cheerful man with a Tom Cruise smile, who tries to remember that it's all just a game. As he emerged from the meeting, he shook his head.

"They are reinventing the wheel in there," he said.

Of course it was possible that the reinvented wheel would work—they had made some pretty good guesses in the past—but the mood of the crew the next morning was grim. Robin, especially, seemed quiet and withdrawn, staring straight ahead with bloodshot eyes. They had decided to make a major gear change, with no way to test it before the race. He blamed himself for being caught in that position.

"I didn't get a lot of sleep," he admitted. "I was too busy worrying about gear ratios."

At about that time, John Wilson walked in. Wilson is the chief engine builder for the team, a quiet, dark-skinned bear of a man with a thin growth of beard and a small wry smile. He is irrepressibly calm, serene almost, in a sport where that is not an easy feat. At the age of forty-three, he has been building engines for three-quarters of his life, and there is a perspective that comes from that kind of experience. Some days are good, some are bad, and all anybody can do is his best.

"There's no use worrying," he told Robin gently. "When it comes to gears, we got what we got."

So the race began with a curious mixture of adrenaline and dread. Kyle Petty once again seemed tight, fretful, as he had in Rockingham—and this time, it didn't take long for his fears to be confirmed. The car ran well for about three laps, but then it quickly began to fade. After eight laps, he had lost a position to Sterling Marlin, and ten laps later to Harry Gant. Hut Stricklin passed him on lap 20, then Alan Kulwicki on lap 21. "I think we killed too much power on this thing," Petty told the crew. They worked desperately to fix it, but nothing helped. The car was slow, and then the handling got worse, and at the halfway point they were three laps down. They were still working hard, still pulling together as a team, but if they kept their poise and self-respect, that was about the only consolation they could find. Petty finished 20th—and only the attrition among other cars kept the ending from being even worse.

After the race, the team leaders gathered—Petty, Robin, John Wilson, Sabates—and they sat for awhile in desolate silence. Petty looked stricken, slumped on a couch, as his eyes that are usually so full of life stared off vacantly at nothing in particular. A year that began with such high hopes, that showed a flash of promise at the Rock, was fast turning bad. Nine days earlier they had won a pole, but now that seemed like a long time ago, and it was hard to even remember how it felt.

At the moment, their car was running with the worst.

The Petty crew was not alone in its bitter frustration. In the trailer next door, Michael Waltrip was beginning to wonder if his luck would ever change. He had finished next to last in Richmond—not because his car was slow, but because they broke a rod bolt worth twenty-eight dollars, and the pieces tore through his engine like a bullet. It was the kind of thing that seemed to happen all the time. In Daytona, he was running 2nd with eight laps to go when he broke a motor—and in the Darlington race the previous spring, he was comfortably in the lead when he pulled in for a final change of tires. All he needed was a routine stop, not even a fast one, and he would win the first race of his Winston Cup career. However, the air wrench failed on his right front tire, and the stop took twice as long as it should have.

For Waltrip, those things are hard to take. He is the younger brother of Darrell Waltrip, who is second in wins among the sport's active drivers. Michael doesn't compare himself to his brother; he knows he came along at a different time, and he knows also that he has made steady progress. He finished second in Pocono in 1988, had four top 5s in 1990, and won two poles in '91. Still, he hungers for that first big win, and when his engine blew apart as it did in Richmond, the emotions for a moment were difficult to manage: "Son of a bitch," he muttered, "this thing blew up." But the time he coasted once around the track, he put on what he called his "PR face."

"Maybe PR is the wrong word," he says. "Maybe it's just being sensitive to other people's feelings. The guys on the team have worked endless hours, and there have been times when I've gone out and torn the car all to hell. They don't go on the TV and say, 'Michael Waltrip doesn't know how to drive.' This is a team sport, and you have to remember it. There are things to consider before you open your mouth."

Besides, says Waltrip, you get used to it—or at least you come to a painful understanding. Racing is a sport that will break your heart. You work as hard as you can and struggle, and the moment of triumph is out there calling. But there are so many categories of disappointment—and some are even worse than a broken rod bolt.

Alan Kulwicki proved that point. In Richmond, he was gaining steadily on the leader, Bill Elliott, and they were side by side in the final turn. But after a wild ride down the front straightaway, Kulwicki's car didn't quite have enough. He lost the race by less than two feet.

Kulwicki, ordinarily, was not a sympathetic figure: He had been on the Winston Cup scene for six years, and by his own admission he didn't have a lot of friends. He was an outsider in a world that can be close-knit—a Wisconsin native who was working on his master's degree in engineering when he decided to go full-time into racing. Nearly everyone agreed he was a talented driver, intelligent and clean, but a lot of people found him condescending and cold. There were times when he could be ungrateful with his crew, aloof and unfriendly in his dealings with the press, and as Kyle Petty once said, he never seemed to be having any fun.

In Richmond, however, you had to feel for him. He faced the cameras in his moment of defeat, brave and gracious as he praised Bill Elliott and the members of his team. "They knew we were there today," he said. "Maybe I should be happy with second." Then his voice choked off, his eyes were red, and for a moment it looked as if Kulwicki might cry, until he gathered himself as he knew he must, and uttered the creed of every driver in the sport: "There's another race next week," he said.

"We'll be back."

CHAPTER 3

ATLANTA TO DARLINGTON: BACK ON TRACK

In Atlanta, they decided to rock 'n' roll. In the first sixty-four days of the year, the Petty crew had spent a half million dollars—which was not exorbitant if you had something to show. Unfortunately their first three races were bad to mediocre, and they had to do something to break out of the gloom. They knew every season is a roller-coaster ride, full of highs and lows and high-speed turns, and the trick was finding a way to stay cool. In Atlanta, they drank.

On Friday night, after Petty qualified 15th for the race on Sunday, Robin, Kyle, Seidenspinner and Felix made the rounds of the uptown bars. Alan Kulwicki was with them for a while—late as usual. He was the kind of guy who would invite himself along, then make you wait. Even that didn't dampen the fun, and about two o'clock, they came to a place that had a bocci ball court on the deck outside. Kyle was ecstatic. To many Americans, the game is a hybrid—a puzzling mixture of shuffleboard and bowling, with two or three rules that resemble horseshoes. Petty had played it fairly often at the beach, but this was Atlanta in March, which meant it was freezing. Seidenspinner noticed there was ice in his beer, but they played anyway for the next several hours, and the next day at the track they were in a better mood. Even the car was starting to come around. In the morning practice, they were a little bit faster than Geoff Bodine, who is usually good, and in the afternoon they were running with Terry Labonte. "I'm as pleased with that as anything we've done in a month," said Robin. "I think we've finally got it in some kind of range."

They settled back after practice to watch the Busch race—a pre-liminary event, which featured, as always, a combination of major-league drivers like Dale Earnhardt and Ernie Irvan, along with others who are on their way up. This particular race was exciting enough, but it was marred by an eight-car wreck coming out of turn 1. Ernie Irvan, once again, was right in the middle—and though everyone agreed it was not his fault, he took quite a lick. His collarbone snapped, the first major injury of his Winston Cup career, and a few people whispered there was justice in that. Irvan, after all, had been responsible for his share of wrecks, including the one in Talladega that injured Kyle Petty. "Swervin' Irvan," the sportswriters called him, and there were drivers who shunned him as he walked through the garage.

Kyle Petty, however, was not among them. He never thought of Irvan as dirty or mean, the kind to wreck another driver on purpose. His mistakes were a matter of terrible judgment, and after Talladega, as soon as Petty could get around on crutches, he made it a point to seek Ernie out. Michael Waltrip remembers the scene: "It was before one of the races in Charlotte," he says, "and it was the first time Kyle was back in the garage. He came over to where Ernie and his crew were working on the car, and Ernie said some-thing like, 'Man, I hate what happened.' Kyle just told him, 'It ain't no big deal, don't worry about it.' "

For months after that, Waltrip puzzled over what he had seen. He knew that Irvan was telling the truth—he hadn't meant to hurt Petty or anybody else, but his apology was late. He hadn't been around to visit Petty in the hospital—hadn't even called him to talk

on the phone. Their encounter in Charlotte came at Petty's insti-
gation, and Waltrip still wasn't sure what it meant. Did Petty really
believe it was not a big deal? Was he offering forgiveness? Or was
it his way of saying, go to hell?

The answer to those questions came clearly in Atlanta. After the
Busch race and the day's final practice, Petty announced to Felix
Sabates that they had a stop to make on the way to the hotel. "We
need to go by and see Ernie," he said. Sabates was appalled. With
the wreck at Talladega, Irvan had destroyed their '91 season and
hadn't even offered a decent apology. Yet Petty insisted, and they
made their way to the Riverdale Hospital, south of Atlanta.

When they arrived, Irvan was lying with an ice pack on his
shoulder, his arm in a sling and the morphine just beginning to
drip. His crew was with him, and a few members of his family,
and the room fell silent as Petty walked in. Sabates followed a
step or two behind, nodding stiffly. They didn't stay long, just
chatted a minute or two, then left. Irvan was groggy and barely
able to talk, but even through his fog he felt a combination of
gratitude and shame. He had known all along when Petty was
hurt that he should have gone by the hospital to see him. He *had*
touched base through Tony Glover, his own crew chief, who had
once spent a year at Petty Enterprises. But Ernie was too embarrassed to go himself, too unsure of what he should say, and there
was something about the hospital that made him afraid. This was
hard to admit, but he told one reporter a couple of weeks later,
"You don't want to see another driver that's hurt. You realize
how dangerous this sport can be."

When the pain subsided and he was able to think, Irvan began
to sort through his guilt, and he finally sat down and wrote Petty
a note. "Dear Kyle," he said. "I never knew how much it meant
for someone to call or come by and see you at the hospital. Sorry
I never called or came by to see you. I know now . . . I am sorry.
Hope we can be friends for a long time. Ernie."

When the note arrived, Petty read it several times and smiled.
He knew it couldn't have been easy to write, but there it was—a
vindication of his instincts and his judgment of Ernie, and a reminder of something about their sport. Racing was dangerous and
bad things happened, but there was never any future in holding a

grudge. They were like a family in that way, thrust together in circumstances that were sometimes hard. When the chips were down, there were no better friends than those he had made in the NASCAR garage.

On the track, of course, you didn't think about it. You had to shove everything out of your mind, and for Petty that began on the morning of the race. Atlanta was no exception. He was feeling the pressure after two bad runs. They had dropped to 14th in the season's point standings, and there was danger that the morale of the team would fade. Inside, however, he was a little more confident than he had been in Richmond. He felt at home on the Atlanta Speedway—a well-designed oval of a mile and a half, almost round, with long, sweeping turns that were steeply banked at 24 degrees. You could go fast there, and in recent years, Petty had been strong. He had a couple of top 5 finishes and two more top 10s, and their Saturday practice this week was encouraging.

On Sunday morning, he was ready. It was a cloudy day, with gusts of wind coming out of the north, while overhead, a small plane circled with a banner behind it: GOOD LUCK, BILL! FROM THE DAWSONVILLE POOL ROOM. It was a hometown plug for driver Bill Elliott, who hadn't seemed to need a lot of luck. He had already won two of the first three races—at Rockingham and then again at Richmond—and once again he was starting near the front.

Petty was not. He had a mediocre qualifying run on Friday, and was starting 15th. When the race began, though, he knew immediately he was going to be fast. He began to pick his way through the field, weaving in and out, passing the slower cars like Ted Musgrave's. He was running 11th after 13 laps, and by lap 35 he was passing Bill Elliott to move up to 9th. All of a sudden there was trouble on the track. Ken Schrader spun coming out of turn 3, and was sliding backwards in a blinding cloud of smoke. Petty was in the middle of an eight-car pack—a dangerous place to be with a wreck just ahead. Luckily all of them made it through this time, passing Schrader on the high side of the track, and they immediately began to pit for new tires.

As he skidded to a stop, Petty studied the movements of his crew. Their pit stops were getting better all the time, as each man settled into his role. Robin Pemberton was the front tire changer;

that was his style, to lead by example. He would jump the wall as Petty pulled in, followed by the others. Mike Ford was the jack man, working first on the right—lifting the car as Robin loosened the front lug nuts, and Jim Sutton did the same on the rear. Jim Long was standing by with new tires, and as soon as Robin and Sutton had them in place, Ford dropped the jack and all of them rushed to the other side. Already, Barry Cook had loosened the lug nuts, front and back, and Richard Bostic with his safety suit and helmet, which made him look like a man from outer space, was beginning to fill the car up with gas.

That was the way it was supposed to go, and if they did it just right, they could change four tires, gas the car, and maybe even make an adjustment in the chassis—all in less than twenty seconds. On this particular stop, however, it was clear to Kyle Petty that something was wrong. The seconds ticked away as Robin struggled with the right front tire. His face was flushed, intense; his eyes were wide and his mouth was set in a taut, thin line. Petty guessed that a lug nut was jammed, but whatever it was they were losing precious time. Robin banged on his wrench several times, then looked relieved, and finally rushed to change the left side tires. By the time they were finished, their pit stop had lasted nearly forty-two seconds.

Petty, who had battled his way from 15th to 9th, was now 25th, and as he roared away to join the field, Robin kicked at a tire and swore beneath the rumble of the engines going past. Nobody mentioned the problem on the radio, as there was no need to talk about it now. It was just one of those things that happened in a race, and Petty's voice on the radio was calm: "We're gonna be all right," he said.

As if to prove himself right, he began to fight his way through the cars, passing Musgrave three abreast and then taking aim on Derrike Cope. Within a few laps, he was back to 18th and bearing down on Rusty Wallace. "Good job," said John Wilson calmly. "You're working right through. You're just about the fastest thing out there."

As always, there was something reassuring about Wilson's tone. His greatest skill on the team was building engines, but he also had an understanding of people—an instinctive gift for the well-timed word. In addition to that, he shared Robin Pemberton's view of their driver. Kyle, they knew, was a confident guy, cocky almost when you saw him at the track. Most of the time he was smiling or telling funny stories, and he never seemed to mind being the center of attention. But there were ways in which his personality was a mask. He was an ambitious man when it came to his work, hard on himself when he made a mistake and blasé on the surface whenever he did well. He didn't seem to need a lot of praise or reassurance, and often when it came he would quickly laugh it off. Robin and John both knew it was an act. "The kid needs it like anybody else," Robin said. "People tend to overlook that about him, I guess because he's so self-assured."

Pemberton and Wilson seldom made that mistake, and their praise came easily as Petty made his way through the traffic in Atlanta, passing Rusty Wallace and Dale Earnhardt, and then Bill Elliott a few laps later. By lap 84, he was running 11th, and after a good pit stop he was all the way to 9th. For the next two hundred laps, there were ebbs and flows with Petty running solidly in the top 10. He was as high as second on lap 175, following their best pit stop of the season—just over nineteen seconds to change four tires and fill the car up with gas. A hundred laps later, he was still in 5th place, when suddenly there was a turning point in the race.

Alan Kulwicki was 4th and fading in a hurry. He decided to pit for new tires, and the other top cars immediately followed suit. They didn't want Kulwicki to gain an advantage. The lone exception was Bill Elliott who decided to stay on the track for another few laps. With the top dozen cars all heading for the pits, Elliott saw a chance to lead the race temporarily—and it was always possible they would catch a caution, which would enable him to pit without losing ground. At that moment it happened. With Kulwicki and the others just returning to the track, Mike Wallace spun and hit the wall. The caution flags came out, which meant that nobody was allowed to pass, and Elliott was now a full lap ahead.

"That damn Georgia boy," muttered Robin Pemberton, "has got the whole field a lap down."

With only forty-one laps to go in the race, it was too much ground for the others to make up, and Elliott simply coasted home for the win. His car was nowhere near the fastest on the track, and when he faced the cameras and accepted the kisses of the pretty girls in Victory Lane, his lopsided smile was more sheepish than usual. "Pure luck," he admitted. "The horseshoe fell out of somebody else's car and fell into mine. That's all I can say."

Kyle Petty, who finished 8th, also smiled and shook his head. It was true that Elliott's luck was annoying, but in another way, you had to be happy for him. Elliott had such a brilliant gift as a driver—a ballet dancer's grace on the track—and he was smart and careful, and you knew you could trust him. As a person he was often misunderstood. He was popular with the fans with his little-boy grin and carrot-blond hair, but he didn't have a lot of friends among the drivers, and he had even fewer among the journalists— they found him aloof and uncommunicative, and it was an image that coincided precisely with success. Elliott began his Winston Cup career in 1976, and didn't win a race for the first eight years. That changed in 1985, when he won eleven, and stardom came in such a rush that by his own admission he was not prepared for it. He won the Daytona 500, the Winston 500 in Talladega, and at the end of that summer he was racing for a million dollar bonus in Darlington. That was the amount put up by Winston for any driver who could win three of the four biggest races in a year.

Elliott won the million dollars, the only driver ever to do it, but he resented the media intrusions on his time. Before the '85 race in Darlington he roped off his car, and stationed a couple of South Carolina highway patrolmen to keep the army of reporters at bay. It was shocking in a sport where driver accessibility is legend. Darrell Waltrip, standing nearby, was battling Elliott for the season championship, and he couldn't resist the opportunity to goad. He grabbed a rag and began to polish his car, telling the assembled reporters with a wink: "You all go on now and leave me alone. I want to work on my race car. Go on now, and leave me alone."

Elliott was bewildered by the whole ordeal. The truth was, he was a shy and introverted man who loved machines, and sometimes had a difficult time with people. He once told a *Charlotte Observer* reporter that if he ever had a week or a few days to himself, he knew what he would do: "Go as far away as I could and hide." His hobbies were individual sports like skiing, and the thing he loved about being a driver was not the speed or the competition or the crowds. It was making the car do exactly what he wanted. "I've always loved cars," he said. "If I had my way, that's all I'd do."

Unfortunately, however, there was more to Elliott's profession than that, and he continued to struggle for the next several years. He won only two races in 1986, and only one each in 1990 and '91. There were also personal problems and tragedy. He filed for divorce in 1990, and later that year his crew member and friend, Mike Rich, was killed in an accident at the Atlanta Speedway. Rich was changing a tire on Elliott's car, when Ricky Rudd hit a patch of oil and spun out of control coming down the pit road. Rich was crushed between the two cars.

Two years later, Elliott bit his lip and looked away when a reporter asked him about the accident. "You have to put a lot of things out of your mind," he said. "That doesn't make the pain go away."

Kyle Petty understood Elliott's pain, and he was glad to see, in 1992, that Elliott was more cheerful than he had been in years. He was winning again, and driving for the legendary owner, Junior Johnson. "You have to be happy for Bill," said Petty. "A lot of people have misunderstood him, but he's a good guy."

His success, however, was beginning to make the rest of them nervous.

They had a week off after the race in Atlanta, and Petty spent the time at his home in High Point, North Carolina. There was only one interruption. The four major Pontiac drivers on the circuit—Kyle and Richard Petty, Michael Waltrip and Rusty Wallace—asked for a meeting with NASCAR officials. So far in a season now four races old, Pontiacs were the slowest cars on the track. It had not always been that way. Wallace, for example, had won the championship in 1989, but now he was mired in 23rd place. Kyle Petty was ninth, the highest ranking among the Pontiac drivers, who were beginning to believe there was a problem with the car. They were asking for some changes in the NASCAR rules, something to improve their horsepower and handling—any kind of break to bring them up to speed.

Such meetings are common in the history of the sport, and there is always a hush-hush quality about them. This one, certainly, was no exception. It occurred in an airplane hangar in Charlotte—the top officials of NASCAR, including Gary Nelson and Bill France, Jr., surrounded by the leaders of the Pontiac teams. For the most part, the meeting was cordial, but in the end the drivers came away disappointed. Nelson rejected nearly all of their suggestions. He did agree to a bigger spoiler—that strip of metal across the rear deck lid that helps to create a downforce of air. Maybe, he said, that would improve their handling, but the rule would apply to every make of car.

Kyle Petty shrugged when the meeting was over. He hadn't expected a lot to begin with, and he had more important things on his mind. His youngest son's birthday was fast approaching, and Kyle was proud of Austin Petty, the family violinist and future astronaut. It barely seemed possible that he was ten. The years could slip away so quickly in racing—the seasons were long, and even between races the schedule was demanding. They had learned to cherish those moments at home, just Kyle and the kids and his pretty wife, Pattie. They had been married for thirteen years, and their memories of that time were bittersweet.

Certainly that was true for Pattie, who had lived with the strain of her husband's growing up. Kyle was only seventeen when they met, while she was nearly twenty-five. She was a knockout, slender and blond with a radiant smile, working as a model to get herself through grad school. They happened to meet one day at the track, and Kyle began coming around to visit. They talked a lot and rode horseback, and though she began to look forward to his visits, she was painfully aware that he was too young. She watched him one time when he was working in her barn. He had taken off his shirt, and she noticed there was a single hair on his chest. "I thought, 'My God, he's only a baby.' " But they were friends, not lovers, and that was one of the things she liked. He seemed so different from a lot of men she had dated—he didn't try to push her into having sex. Instead, he was gentle, and he listened in a way that most men didn't, and for about eight months everything was fine. But then one day he looked her in the eye. "I'm in love with you," he said. "I'm going to marry you someday."

She smiles today when she remembers his boldness, but at the moment all she thought was, "Oh my God." She tried to explain that the gap was too wide—he was still in high school, playing football, while she was on the verge of beginning her career. But when he went away and didn't come around for the next several days, she couldn't help but notice she was feeling an ache. One day, he showed up again. "I know I've thrown you for a loop," he said. "I know you don't want what I want. But I wanted you to have this." He handed her a box with a necklace inside, and she felt her resistance give way in a rush.

"I looked into those big brown eyes," she says, "and I just melted. I said, 'I think I love you too.' "

They had some trying times after that. The love story mingled with other parts of life, as she watched him grow up and grapple with fame, and sometimes yearn for the adolescence he had missed. But they stayed together and took it as it came.

Among other things, there were difficult moments in Kyle's career, and for Pattie at least, many of the hardest were in the early years. Kyle was working with his father at Petty Enterprises, and showing some promise. He nearly won his first race in 1982, only his second full year on the circuit, and twice he finished in the top 5. When his father then asked him to run the business as well as drive, the dual assignment proved to be a misery. "His relationship with his dad was falling apart," says Pattie. "Richard wanted him to run the business, then didn't like the way he did it. They were butting heads. Kyle was only twenty-three when he started. It was a very hard time."

For Kyle the worst part of the ordeal was financial. Their sponsorship money was no longer enough, and it was nearly impossible to field two cars—one for Richard and another for his son. Richard decided, in 1984, that he would finally try driving for somebody else; but even then the money was short, and Kyle was having a miserable year on the track. The debts were mounting at Petty Enterprises, and to pay them off, Kyle started selling off chunks of his land. He had more than two hundred acres in the Carolina hills—and now, bit by bit, they could see it shrinking.

It was about that time that they decided to move. They found a lakeside cabin near the Uhwarrie Mountains, and Kyle went to work for the Wood Brothers' team. They paid him $50,000 a year and all he had to do was drive a car. "We thought we had died and gone to heaven," says Pattie—and to make it even better, Kyle started to win: he was first in Richmond in 1986, and won the Coca-Cola 600 the following year—one of the Big Four races in the world of NASCAR. Then when he didn't win at all in 1988 the Wood Brothers asked him to find a new job. They had grown accustomed to being at the top. The great David Pearson had driven for them in the 1970s, winning more races than anybody but Richard Petty, and Neil Bonnett had won an average of two a year after that. The Woods liked Kyle and he liked them, but some people said they doubted his focus, wondered if he was serious enough for the job.

In any case, things were looking bleak when Petty got a call from Felix Sabates. Actually, it was an intermediary at first, asking him to fly to Charlotte for a talk. It was a summer night, well after dark when Petty's plane touched down. A limousine was waiting at the airport for him, and the driver took him around to a darkened hangar, instructing him simply to go inside. Kyle did as he was told, but there was no one there. Alone in the shadows, he began to wonder if it was some kind of joke. Where exactly am I? he thought. And does anybody know? He smiled and shook his head at his own apprehension, and after a few minutes Sabates came in, a handsome man with jet-black hair and a winning smile. The more they talked, the more Petty liked him. Felix was flamboyant and good-humored and wealthy enough to support a good team, but you had to wonder about a man like that. The rich were accustomed to having their way, and racing as a sport could be unpredictable; but Sabates said he understood all that, and within a few weeks they had worked out a deal. The new team struggled in 1989, then started winning races in '90 and '91, and things were going well until the ugly wreck at Talladega.

For Pattie especially, it was a tough one to swallow. The money ran short during the long, hard months of her husband's convalescence. Felix continued to pay his salary, but they missed the winnings he could have earned at the track. More than that, she hated the idea of another setback in a career that had seen its ups and downs. Life could be unfair sometimes. Nevertheless, she was proud of the way Kyle was battling back, first with the weights and rehabilitation and then when he got back into the car. At the Darlington race in the fall of '91, the windshield shattered and sprayed glass in his eye. But he refused to stop, and simply washed out the slivers with a bottle of water.

So far, 1992 had been the same. Everything seemed to make him more determined, but they still didn't have enough to show for it. Atlanta had been an encouraging stop and now their sights were set on Darlington, the Lady in Black, the oldest superspeedway of all. Some of the drivers regarded it with dread. It's an egg-shaped oval built in 1950, when race cars traveled about half as fast. Today they broke 160, even though the asphalt was rough and hard on tires and the steeply banked turns were all very different. If the driver and his crew tried to set up the car for turns 1 and 2, searching for just the right springs and shocks, they sacrificed something in 3 and 4—and those were the most treacherous turns in the sport. The fastest groove was high on the track, and when the drivers raced there, as the best of them did, the centrifugal force would sling them out six inches from the wall. Sometimes it was less, and by the end of the day, a driver who had been both lucky and good would have a black stripe down the side of his car—the Darlington stripe, they liked to call it, a badge of courage, where the wall had scraped away the paint.

On a bad day, of course, it was more than a stripe. Bill Elliott remembers a race in 1986 when he had a big lead with seven laps to go and inexplicably drove straight into the wall. "What happened?" he says. "I have no idea . . . Looking back, I can't think of a thing I did different or wrong."

Such was the legend of the Darlington track—a treacherous place where anything could happen—and the reputation extended even to the crowds. A lot of people said the infield bunch was the toughest anywhere on the NASCAR circuit. There was nothing to disprove it in 1992. "It got a little rowdy here last night," one fan reported on Saturday morning. "And we're not finished yet." Two campers away, where a Confederate flag was snapping in the breeze and t-bone steaks were sizzling on the grill, a boy and his daddy were sizing up the crowd. They were perched unsteadily on the roof of the camper, and the boy, who was ten, was holding out a sign to the women passing by. LET THE PUPPIES BREATHE, it pleaded. That was the poetic rendition of the message—the more literal version was on the other side: SHOW US YOUR TITS.

The women didn't seem offended or surprised, and if none so far had accepted the offer, the boy was hopeful and his daddy was proud—standing there quietly, arms folded at his chest, and a look of expectation in his eyes.

Inside the garage, the mood was more serious, and at the moment, among Kyle Petty's crew it was grim. Somehow, they had set the car on fire. It seems they had a bad spark plug wire and in the process of going into the engine to fix it, they unhooked the gas line and somebody forgot to hook it back. A few seconds later when they started the car, the gas ignited and flames burst out from the motor in a whoosh. They put it out quickly and were searching for damage, when Kyle wandered over to inquire, "Hey guys, anybody got a light?"

Robin smiled in appreciation—it was Petty's way of putting people at ease—but inside he wondered what else could go wrong. On Friday morning they hadn't passed inspection, which meant extra work before they could practice, and on Friday afternoon they qualified 17th. In a way he wasn't too worried about that: in Rockingham and Richmond, they had spent a lot of time trying to qualify fast, and hadn't been ready when it came time to race. From now on, he said, they would avoid that mistake. They spent all of Saturday fine-tuning the car, and by the end of the day they were feeling a little better. "I think we're ready," Robin finally declared, and by race time Sunday it was clear that he was right.

From the moment they started, Kyle's Pontiac was flying. He passed Ken Schrader and Morgan Shepard, then Dale Jarrett and Darrell Waltrip, and he was running 7th after thirteen laps. By lap 25, he was all the way to 4th when Sterling Marlin, who had won the pole, spun and hit the wall directly in front of him. Petty dove low through the smoke from Marlin's car, held his breath in a split-second of dread, then knew he had made it.

"Good move!" exclaimed Steve Knipe, the spotter.

They pitted for tires, and Robin didn't bother to conceal his delight. "You've got a real good car today," he said. "Take care of your stuff. You're doing great, you really are."

For the next fifty laps they were in the top five, battling Earn-hardt and chasing Davey Allison, when the rear end slipped coming out of turn 4. "It's getting a little loose," said Petty. The radio was silent for the next several laps, as he struggled with the car and tried to stay ahead of the others bearing down. One by one they began to pass him—Earnhardt, Elliott, Terry Labonte. "It's bad loose now," he reported, but Robin told him to hang in there.

"It's too early to pit," he said. "We need to go another six laps. Can you deal with it?"

"Ten-four," said Kyle. "I'll be all right . . . just can't hold on to third place."

Six laps later his voice was frayed. "Not much longer, man."

"Rog," said Robin, "pit next time."

It was clear by then that the track was chewing up tires in a hurry, and the car was dangerous when the tires got slick. The obvious answer was to pit more often. Harry Gant had adopted that strategy, never pushing his tires beyond fifty laps, and he was now in a furious battle for the lead. Kyle and Robin decided to follow suit, and for much of the time during the next one hundred laps they had the fastest car on the track. Petty was fourth near the halfway point, when suddenly there was trouble on the track just ahead. Geoff Bodine and Darrell Waltrip ran together. Bodine was fine, but Waltrip hit the wall coming into turn 1.

"Go low, go low!" shouted Steve Knipe. Petty did, and though it was close, once again he made it through unscathed.

As Kyle and the other leaders began to pit for new tires, Wal-trip's crew pushed his Chevrolet to the garage. Waltrip was fuming. He had never had a lot of use for Bodine, and when a TV reporter asked him what happened, he hesitated for a second and then let fly: "There was a little *turd* driving number fifteen that ran all over me."

You could almost hear the announcer's gasp. Drivers say those things all the time, but seldom do they do it on national TV. There are fans to please and sponsors to represent, and tantrums are bad for the image of the sport. Waltrip, however, didn't need to worry. The television boys could tidy things up, talking about emotions running high in the heat of a race, and "turd" is not a word in a family newspaper. Most decided to airbrush it altogether. In the

Charlotte Observer, the biggest daily in the heart of racing country, Waltrip's outburst was rendered in this way: "The guy driving #15 ran all over me."

Kyle Petty would laugh about it later—the reporters could be so soft sometimes—but at the moment he had other things on his mind. They had escaped two wrecks and battled slick tires, but now a more serious problem had appeared. As he studied the panel of gauges on his dash, it was clear to Kyle that his car was overheating. He wondered if the problem was the tape they had placed on the front grillwork. They put it there to cut the flow of air, mostly to improve the aerodynamics, but it also made the engine run hotter.

"You may want to take off a little of the tape," he told the crew. "About an inch per side, ten-four?"

He and Robin both thought it was done, but when he left the pits and returned to the race, the pieces of tape were still on the grill. For the first few laps, everything was fine. Kyle gained quickly on the cars in front, and by lap 200 he was in second place, just a few inches from the bumper of the leader, Davey Allison. Several times it appeared he would pass, but on lap 207 he felt something change. Somehow the power of the engine seemed to fade. He glanced quickly at the gauges on the dash, and the temperatures now were in the danger zone. They pitted to try to cool things down, popping the radiator cap to let off steam. For a while, it worked and he rushed once again toward the front of the field. But on lap 251, with 116 to go in the race, Petty's voice was on the radio again.

"This thing is boiling water," he said. "We're gonna run it till it cooks." The radio was quiet and nobody said anything in the pits. The faces were grim as Petty's voice returned, laughing this time: "We already had it on fire one time. Let's see what happens."

Three minutes later the engine quit for good, and as he reflected on the ruins of a promising afternoon, Robin kept returning to a single thought. What if they had removed the tape from the grill? Maybe it wouldn't have helped. Maybe the pieces of rubber from the tires of other cars, which had splattered on the grill since early in the race, had really done more damage than the tape. Still, the possibilities and what-ifs were maddening. There were a million different ways to lose a race, and you never seemed to win unless everything was right. It was a frustrating, goddamn sport they had chosen. The story did have a bright side to it: they had put an impressive car on the track, and Kyle had driven it with brilliance and skill. There was hope in that. "Surely," Robin said, "it's just a matter of time . . . "

CHAPTER 4

BUMP AND GRIND—SEASON OF THE SHORT TRACKS

Kyle Petty hated the track in Bristol. "It's a hole," he said. "They ought to blow it up."

Actually, it was a pretty exciting place for the fans—a half-mile oval in the Tennessee hills with turns that were banked at 36 degrees. The fastest cars could run a lap in sixteen seconds, and with thirty or thirty-five on the track at one time, spectacular collisions were an everyday occurrence. Bristol wasn't the only place like that. It was merely the beginning of a short track season that some drivers loved and others regarded with a deep sense of dread. Almost *nobody* thought it was dull. Each of these races—at Bristol, North Wilkesboro and Martinsville, Virginia,—was a throwback of sorts, a reminder of small-town Saturday nights where the faithful gathered at the little dirt tracks and the cars banged away and went careening through the turns, and nobody cared too much about finesse.

In 1992, Kyle Petty figured the sheet metal carnage would be even worse. They had put a new coat of pavement on the track at Bristol, which it badly needed, but the result in the testing they had done so far was to push the speeds even higher on a track that was already too fast for its size. To make matters worse, nobody had had enough time to practice. An April snowfall hit the Tennessee hills—as much as six or eight inches in some elevations—and the scheduled practice on Saturday was scratched. The day before, they had qualified 23rd, which meant they were starting near the back on a track where everybody knew it was hard to pass.

"I've been better," groused Robin Pemberton when a reporter asked him how he was doing. Standing nearby on the morning of the race, Barry Cook grinned. He's a stocky and good-humored member of the crew, whose job is to change the left rear tire. When the reporter wanted to know what it would take to make a decent run from the 23rd position, Cook gave a wink and interjected his opinion.

"Big balls," he said. "I think he's got 'em."

For the first few laps, it was hard to tell. Petty was mired near the rear of the field, and he was struggling with the car, which was loose on the turns and pushing in the middle. Still, he was making a little bit of progress when he collided with Bill Elliott on lap 31. "The son of a bitch cut down on me," he yelled. The caution flag came out for a couple of laps and though both cars were able to continue, Elliott clearly got the worst of the encounter. His dented car was never good all day, while Petty's, after a pit stop or two, gradually emerged as one of the contenders.

It was becoming a nerve-wracking pattern by now—fighting through traffic from the back of the pack. It was hard on the driver and hard on the car, but for the last few races it was all they could do. This time it took him about one hundred laps, but after a caution at the fifty-mile mark, he was the 9th-place car and bearing down on Labonte. It was several more laps before he could pass. There was only one fast groove on the track, and to get around another good car you had to ride bumper to bumper for a while, then dive low on the high-banked turns. Sometimes you made it, sometimes you didn't, but he was chipping away and moving up steadily when he began to notice a few problems with the car. For one thing, he was losing his brakes. This was bad when you were traveling at speeds of 120 and everywhere around you the traffic was thick. Petty decided, however, not to say anything to the crew. There was nothing much they could do about it now, not without a long pit stop that would all but obliterate their chances in the race. Besides, the brakes were still working if he pumped them enough, but there was another problem that was even more perplexing. The engine, which had overheated so badly in Darlington, was now running cool.

"If you average it out," joked Petty as he circled the track, "we're perfect both places." Nobody in the pit seemed to think it was funny. The last thing they needed was an engine problem now. Their luck had mostly been rotten all year, and here in Bristol it had started out the same. Still, they had survived one wreck and made it all the way from the back of the pack, and Petty was still passing other cars on the track. By the halfway mark, he was all the way to 5th, chasing Alan Kulwicki as the two of them made their way through the traffic, gaining steadily on the leader, Darrell Waltrip. The radio fell silent now, as it often does in the heat of a race. Petty was focused on the chase, shaving a little off the lead each lap. He had cut it by a second when all of a sudden he hit the wall. At first, nobody on the crew could believe it. Everything was fine; he was running high on the track coming into turn 4, when he hit a spot where the tires of other cars had torn up the asphalt. It was like driving abruptly from pavement to gravel, and his car lurched wildly and skidded to the right. It hit the wall and bounced away, then hit again with such force that it almost flipped. Petty wasn't hurt, but his voice on the radio was forlorn. "Sorry about that, man."

They were able to fix it, but it took twenty laps to replace the fuel pump and pull the bent sheet metal out of the way. Amazingly enough, they were still pretty fast, passing other cars all the way to the end. But they had lost a lot of time, and finished 19th.

"Nice job," said Robin. "You hung in there." Petty was in no mood for compliments. "Where do you want this thing?" he snapped, referring to the battered car he was driving.

In the gloom that followed, it fell to John Wilson to put things in perspective. "This is short track racing," he said. "Things just happen."

His voice, as always, sounded serene.

The following week, it was North Wilkesboro. If ever a track fit the stereotype of racing, this one did. The speedway itself had once been dirt, with cars power-sliding into the turns and roaring out again in a shower of clay. NASCAR had been there since the 1940s and when the asphalt came in '57, the speeds picked up and the crowds grew larger, but everything else seemed pretty much the same. The grandstand was nestled in the hills of Wilkes County, the hard scrabble fringe of the Appalachian mountains, where there is a curious intermingling of poverty and new wealth. Just around the curve from tin-roofed houses and unpainted barns and double-wide trailers that are beginning to rust, there are A-frame houses of cedar and stone with palomino horses grazing in front. Life can still be hard in these outback stretches of North Carolina: years ago, it was moonshine country, where people did whatever they could to survive, and some folks say there is still white lighting available in the hills. In 1992, nobody at the track seemed to think it was strange when they decided to honor the most famous bootlegger of all.

Junior Johnson, of course, was no longer in the business. He was a car owner now, one of the most respected men in his sport, fielding teams for Bill Elliott and Sterling Marlin, but as a much younger man he had learned to drive while running moonshine in the hills of Wilkes County. It was a brutal life as he looked back on it: dodging liquor agents on the steep mountain roads, getting up at all hours no matter what the weather—sleet, snow, it didn't make any difference—and traipsing off through the hollows to check on the mash. He was glad to give it up to drive a race car. He told Tom Wolfe, in an article for *Esquire*, that he was plowing in his garden one day in Wilkes County when a couple of local boys persuaded him to race. They went down to a little dirt track in the hills, and Junior came in 2nd his first time out. From that moment on, he says he was hooked.

He won fifty races at the Winston Cup level, which put him 8th on the list all-time, and people still talk about the way he drove.

Junior was a banger, famous for his duels with Lee Petty and others. He was almost spooky in his physical courage, careening in and out of the turns, but he was also involved in some important innovations. He discovered one time on a practice run at Daytona that if he ran nose to tail with the car just ahead, he could keep up easily even when he knew the other guy was faster. It made sense, of course. The first car punched a hole in the air, and the second had less to hold it back. None of that mattered when you were sliding through the turns on a quarter-mile track. But with the rise of superspeedways in the 1960s, all the great drivers made the same discovery—racing was physics as much as raw nerve, and if you were going to compete, you had to get serious about the technology.

More and more, that meant a lot of money, which eventually meant turning to corporate sponsors. The sport kept changing, and some people didn't like it, but Johnson was smart enough to adjust. When he gave up driving to run his own team, a move he made in 1966, he began to wean himself from the day-to-day business of running the car. "I do miss it," he admits today. "But my time is focused on development work—the stuff that makes us winners down the line. I'm an innovator. I try to stay on top of what's coming down the road. It's interesting. You do some crazy things."

His flexibility showed clearly in his choice of drivers, whose styles sometimes were not at all like his own. Bill Elliott was a prime example. He had made his reputation on patience and finesse, while Junior was known for his aggressiveness and courage. Yet when a reporter asked if he would try to change Elliott's style, Junior simply smiled and stared at him hard. "You make a grave mistake," he said, "questioning other people's judgment."

On April 12, 1992, just before the race, they were paying tribute to Johnson for all that—for being a winner and a link to the past, but also for being a symbol of change. He stood there stiffly and accepted their cheers, hands folded quietly behind his back. "I am proud to be here for this honor," he said. "I can't tell you what it means to me."

Then he stepped aside and it was time to race.

There had been a lot of talk about Davey Allison. He had hit the wall pretty hard in Bristol, hurting his ribs, and he was racing this week in a special flak jacket. There was also talk about Alan Kulwicki, who won the race in Bristol and the North Wilkesboro pole. Almost nobody was talking about Petty; he had faded all the way to 15th in points and hadn't come close to winning a race, and already at Wilkesboro his season-long pattern of ups and downs continued. He qualified 15th on Friday, not so much because he was slow—halfway through the round, he was one of the fastest. Then a cloud came over and cooled the track, and eight straight cars—eleven in all—were able to beat his time by a fraction.

On Saturday in practice, the transmission didn't work and for the people on the crew who were inclined to superstition, there was a worrisome thought somewhere in their minds. For the first time since Richmond they were running The Duke. Most of them tried to be rational about it. Jane Gossage, who handles PR, pointed out that the car had done quite well in the past, never mind the debacles at Rockingham and Richmond. Kyle himself was even more emphatic. "When the ball doesn't go in the hoop," he said, "you don't change balls." Besides, there had been a couple of good signs on Saturday. After they got the transmission fixed, they ran about 30 practice laps in a row. The car was fast and seemed to get stronger, and Robin was smiling at the end of the day. "I think we'll be all right," he said.

When the race began, it was touch and go. Petty was patient, trying to stay out of trouble. The track was starting to get slick in a hurry, and after seven laps they had the first spin. Dale Jarrett lost it coming out of turn 4, and when the cars just behind him hit the brakes, Richard Petty plowed into them both. The front end of Richard's car was destroyed—a reminder to the field that it could be a long day at North Wilkesboro.

For Kyle, however, things began to go well. After the caution, he started passing cars, and by about lap 40 his Mello Yello Pontiac was the fastest thing on the track. "You're running down the leader," Robin Pemberton told him, and for the next thirty laps he moved up quickly. He passed Bill Elliott and Harry Gant, and on lap 71 he was all the way to 8th. He made it to 7th by lap 89, and twenty laps later he was in the middle of a three-way battle for 6th. Davey Allison was just ahead, and Petty was on his bumper trying to pass. He dove low and Allison cut down to block his path, faked high and Allison swerved up to block him again. It was a replay of old battles between their fathers, Bobby and Richard, and for a dozen laps the pattern continued—Petty in a car that was obviously faster trying to pass on a track with one groove. Finally, he made it, or so he thought. He dove low coming out of turn 1 and made it to the door of Allison's Ford before Davey cut down and drove him to the grass. It was an irritating habit that Allison had developed—cutting down on people with a clear line to pass—and Petty decided he had had enough. He let his car drift up a few feet, and when the two cars bumped Allison lost control and spun to the grass. He missed the wall and the oncoming traffic, and both cars were able to stay in the race. In the short run, Petty gained a spot while Allison fell back to the middle of the pack. "I got all the way to his door," Petty snapped, but Robin's voice on the radio was calm: "It's an accident," he said. "It happens."

Petty held onto 6th for the next forty laps, but he started slipping on lap 170. His tires were worn and his car was loose, and for the first time in the race he was clearly losing ground. Geoff Bodine passed him low, and Morgan Shepherd high. Petty was eighth and hoping for a caution, when, sure enough, Wally Dallenbach hit the wall. They pitted for new tires and tightened the chassis, and did it all so fast that Petty gained two positions on the stop. "That was a great pit stop!" he said. "A *great* stop, guys." The problem was, they got the car too tight, and the race was a struggle for the next hundred laps. At one point Petty was running as high as third; at another he faded all the way to 12th. He was 11th when he had his second wreck of the day. He was a couple of car lengths behind Ernie Irvan, when Irvan hit a patch of loose asphalt. He had to slow down, and Petty couldn't stop and hit him from the rear.

"He stopped, and I hit him. It was my fault," Petty told the crew.

Both cars were able to continue—Irvan's with a fair-sized dent in the rear, while Petty's, remarkably, was nearly unscathed. The next time, however, he was not so lucky. He was battling for 10th on lap 290, running as fast as the leader, Rusty Wallace, when he found himself in a duel with Bobby Hillin. Petty was surprised. Hillin is not a top driver on the circuit, though there was a time in his career when he showed great promise. He won Talladega at age twenty-two, and some people thought he could be the next star. He was good-looking and smart, a quiet Texas boy with sandy-blond hair and ice-blue eyes and a rodeo rider's demeanor and physique. As a driver, though, Hillin never cashed in on his promise. His first and only win was six years earlier, and everybody knew his career was on the skids. In 1992, he was a part-time driver on an underfunded team, and he occasionally filled in for others who were hurt. The year before, when Petty broke his leg, Hillin took his place for eight races—never finishing in the top 10. At North Wilkesboro, he was replacing Chad Little, a driver who was fired the week before. Like anybody struggling in that position, Hillin was determined to make a good impression. He was down a lap when he and Kyle Petty began to tangle, and he was battling desperately to make up the ground. He refused to give ground when Petty went around him, and a few laps later passed him back. Petty had his mind on more important things—he was battling Morgan Shepherd for 11th position and gaining on Brett Bodine for tenth. Hillin, at most, was a minor irritant—a driver who was seldom in contention anymore—and Petty ducked low to pass him again.

For the next six laps Hillin stayed on his bumper, and when he couldn't get around on lap 311, he did something incredible. He clipped the rear of Petty's Pontiac and sent it spinning backwards into the wall. It wasn't Hillin's style to wreck people on purpose, but the move seemed flagrant to NASCAR officials and they hit him immediately with a five-lap penalty. It was one of the stiffest punishments of the year, but the damage to Petty was already done. His car was stalled in the middle of the track, and it wasn't hard to tell that the problem was serious.

"I can't get it cranked," Petty told the crew.

"Is there a wrecker close by?" Robin wanted to know.

"Nah, man, there's nobody here."

Felix Sabates had heard enough. He cut loose a torrent of Cuban profanity, and charged off in a rage to Bobby Hillin's pit. He jumped the wall and kicked Hillin's car and screamed something at him that was lost in the roar. Dick Seidenspinner was standing nearby, and if he couldn't quite hear all the words, he didn't have any doubt that they were colorful. Felix was never known for his even disposition, and at this particular moment he felt betrayed. He had given Hillin a job the year before, and now the son of a bitch had wrecked them.

On the track, meanwhile, Petty was also beginning to fume. They had managed to get the car running again, but it was limping along, easily the slowest thing out there. "Just be cool," Robin told him gently, but Petty's voice on the radio was firm. "I'm gonna be cool . . . and I'm gonna take care of Hillin."

Nothing else happened until the end of the race. Petty disembarked and talked a while with the guys on the crew. They went over what worked and didn't work in the race, then Petty got up and ambled away. Nobody paid a lot of attention—he didn't seem angry or upset anymore; but when he got to the other side of the NASCAR garage, he veered in the direction of Bobby Hillin's truck, where a lone crew member was working on the car.

"Where's Hillin?"

The crew member, a burly young man with a grease smudge coating the side of his face, looked up uncertainly and gave no reply. Petty shrugged and pointed a finger toward the crew member's face. "You bring that motherfucker back to the race track . . . you won't be able to roll the car on the truck. That's a promise." Then he turned and walked away.

It was something, he knew, that his father might have done, though maybe with a different choice of words. Richard generally was a little more patient, but there were times: the season before, he had confronted the driver Bobby Hamilton after Hamilton, a rookie, had spun him in a race. The King didn't appreciate the lack of respect. "Don't jack with me," he said, staring hard into Hamilton's eyes. "I'll do it four times worse to you." Kyle remembers that Hamilton got the message.

"A lot of people talk about intimidation," he says. "The King does it in the truck, where nobody sees it."

But intimidation is only part of it, and at North Wilkesboro, Petty had another piece of business on his mind. He felt bad about running into Ernie Irvan, who had finished a disappointing 13th. The wreck was one of the main reasons why, so Kyle made his way from Hillin's truck to Irvan's, where he offered his apology face-to-face. Irvan accepted with a smile, and Petty went back to rejoin his own crew.

"We're not finishing for shit," he told them. "But we're running good. We keep putting on a pretty good show."

At Martinsville, Virginia, they tried it again, and despite the bad luck of the past three races—two devastating crashes and an engine failure—they were feeling pretty good about their chances. Kyle did well on the Martinsville Speedway, the shortest and slowest track on the circuit. It was set in the hills of southern Virginia, neatly landscaped with rows of dogwood lining the entrance. By race week they were all in bloom, pinks and whites everywhere you looked, and the setting was serene, except for what was happening out on the track.

The Martinsville course is a hard one to drive—two short straightaways of eight hundred feet, dragstrips essentially, with short flat turns at either end. Speeds in the turns could drop to sixty and nearly double again down the stretch. It was hard on the motor with dramatic changes in the RPMs, and harder still on the brakes, and some drivers found it hard on the nerves. Kyle, however, seemed to like it. He had finished second the year before in a race that he came very close to winning.

Partly on the basis of that success, they decided to go with The Duke once again. It had served them well in '91, and was running okay in North Wilkesboro until Bobby Hillin struck. They discovered the damage was worse than they thought, but the crew worked hard—putting in at least one hundred extra hours—replacing essentially the entire rear end. Robin was proud of what they had done, and hoping for good things on the first day of practice. From the start, however, the car was temperamental. It was maddeningly slow the first time out, and only a little better when they changed the gears. That afternoon, they qualified 17th—which meant, once again, they'd be starting near the back. Their frustration was building when they practiced on Saturday, but finally they began to see a little hope. They tinkered some more with the gears and the chassis, and by the middle of the day they were running pretty fast.

In late afternoon they went out again, just to test the last bit of fine-tuning. Robin was smiling, hoping for the best, but lap after lap the times were appalling. They huddled desperately to figure it out—Robin, Kyle and the engine builder, John Wilson—and the scary thing was, they didn't have a clue. "We're out there lost," Petty said with a laugh, "trying to get back."

Meanwhile, back home, Felix Sabates was going through the roof. He had planned to skip this particular race, spending the time on his yacht off Hilton Head Island. But when he heard they had qualified 17th, the Cuban Tornado went out of control. He called his pilots and told them they were going to Martinsville after all. He also told them not to tell anyone. He planned to show up at the track unannounced.

It was an ugly scene when Sabates finally arrived. All morning long he was huddled with one person or another, complaining angrily about the failures of his team. One of those people was Gary Nelson, Petty's crew chief from the season before, who was now the chief inspector for NASCAR. Nelson listened with a patient smile, as Felix shook his head and jabbed at the air with his right forefinger. "They'll turn it around," Nelson told him finally. "Keep working at it." A few minutes later, Nelson found Robin Pemberton and told him simply to hang in there.

Robin, however, was feeling the heat. He could understand Sabates' frustration; he felt it himself, but he was hurt and angry at the sudden lack of confidence. That same Sunday morning, Sabates had jumped him outside the truck, and there was nothing too small to escape his rage. Among other things, Felix was furious that Richard Bostic, the veteran truck driver for the Petty team, had failed to stock the truck with Ultra Slimfast, which Sabates liked to drink before a race. Robin listened, tried to explain, then finally gave up and listened some more.

In his previous job as crew chief for Mark Martin, he had clashed off and on with the temperamental owner of the team, Jack Roush. Maybe it was one of the hazards of the business. Maybe all owners were really that way, but it was more than Robin wanted to put up with, and he took his new job hoping and believing that Sabates was different. Certainly, he knew, Felix was generous and anything but aloof, and whenever he was pleased he let people know it. But Sabates was a man who was feeling the pressure. His team was on a pace to spend maybe $3.5 million for the season—most of it money put up by the sponsors—and so far they didn't have much to show for it. Nobody, of course, could dispute that conclusion, and Robin did his best to understand. But there was also a troubling thought in his mind, rumbling around somewhere in the back; When people are working as hard as they can, doing everything they know how to do, what good does it do to demand even more? He didn't understand why Felix couldn't see it, and in the last few minutes before the race, Robin's mood was as grim as it had been all year. He was hoping desperately they would have a good race.

For the first few laps, it didn't look good. They faded immediately from 17th to 21st, tried to be patient while the other cars wrecked, which seemed to happen about every five laps. The Duke was loose, not sticking to the turns, but again and again Petty made it through the trouble. By about lap 40, the car felt better, just as it had in North Wilkesboro, and now he was picking his way through the field. He passed Hut Stricklin and then Rick Mast, and every time around he was faster than the leader. "You're doing it, man," Robin said from the pit.

Petty made it to 11th by lap 100, and he was gaining on Sterling Marlin for 10th. The tension was beginning to ease in the pit; every now and then somebody would smile. The car was running so fast right now, it was hard to imagine it wouldn't be a good day. But ten laps later, Petty's voice was forlorn. "The left rear tire is flat," he said.

They had to pit while everybody else was running full speed, and before they knew it they were a full lap down. Actually, it was almost worse than that. Alan Kulwicki was leading the race, and he was bearing down quickly as Petty left pit road. If Kulwicki passed, they'd be two laps behind, and their chances of a win would all but disappear. Kyle was determined to hold him off, and for the next fifty laps it was quite a battle—both cars weaving in and out of the traffic, both clearly faster than anyone else. Robin hoped Felix was paying attention. It was true that the flat had put them in a hole, but it was also obvious that they had a good car. With any kind of luck . . . but on lap 180, they blew another tire. Robin looked stricken, wondering how things could get any worse—and then they did. When the tire blew out, Petty came close to losing control, as he slid down low to the apron of the track. He stopped to let the leaders go by, and NASCAR penalized him two laps. They said he caused a caution unnecessarily.

With the penalty and two flats, they were now about five laps off the pace, and still their car was one of the fastest. Petty could feel the brakes getting soft—"You have to pump 'em," he told the crew—but he was still pushing hard, still creeping back toward a decent finish. They were in 15th position with forty laps to go, when the brakes failed completely and he hit the wall.

This time he hit it hard. He broke the gas line and dumped fuel on the track, and a shower of sparks erupted from the crash. The gasoline began to burn like a fuse.

"Are you okay?" asked Robin Pemberton.

For an agonizing moment, there was no reply. Finally, Petty's voice sounded tired and resigned. "I'm okay, I'm okay."

Robin looked relieved, but only for a moment. "That thing is burning underneath you," he said—and indeed the fire was getting bigger all the time.

Inside the car, Petty was struggling with his shoulder harness. He couldn't see the flames, and it hadn't really occurred to him yet to worry. But across the track, they could see more clearly. The fire was building and he was still in the car, and there was no sign yet that he was going to get out.

Geoff Bodine was one of those watching, and it occurred to him suddenly that something horrible was happening. Bodine was already out of the race; he had blown an engine early in the day, and now he was a spectator on pit row, directly across from where Petty crashed.

Bodine and Petty go back a long way. When Geoff, a New Yorker, came south to join the circuit, Kyle was one who made him feel welcome. Not everybody did. Some people found him hard to work with—a perfectionist, demanding on himself and the crew— while others simply saw him as a permanent outsider. Not Petty. He liked Bodine for his decency and wit, and the two of them were friendly almost from the start. None of this mattered at the moment, however. Bodine simply saw a disaster in the making—a trail of gas, a shower of sparks and a driver having trouble getting out of the car. "I said, 'Please, please don't catch fire.' " But the blaze was building and Petty seemed trapped.

Without really thinking about what he was doing, Bodine grabbed a fire extinguisher from the pit and bolted toward the track. He glanced quickly to his right at the oncoming traffic—the race was already under caution, of course, but the cars were still traveling at more than 60 m.p.h. He couldn't run out in front of just anybody, but to his great relief, he saw Mark Martin leading the pack—a driver he knew he could trust to slow down.

By now, Petty's car was on the edge of exploding. Flames were billowing from under the hood, and Bodine was sure that if they got any bigger, the fire extinguisher wouldn't be enough. He took a deep breath and ran across the track.

Meanwhile, a few feet away in Wally Dallenbach's pit, Tony Liberati couldn't believe what he was seeing. A former marine, Liberati is a mechanic who got his start with Richard Petty. He liked and admired the whole Petty family, and now here was Kyle in a burning car. Liberati could see him trying to climb out, but he slid back down and Tony knew immediately what the problem had to be. Like most drivers on the Martinsville track, where the turns are sharp and come so often, Petty had strapped his helmet to the shoulder harness. It kept his neck from whiplashing to the side—but until he could get that strap unhooked he wouldn't be able to get out of the car. Liberati could see that he needed some help, and he bolted across the track with Bodine.

They made it to the car at about the same time. Bodine turned the fire extinguisher loose on the blaze and within a few seconds the fire was out. Liberati, meanwhile, pulled Petty from the car. It had been thirty-eight seconds since the crash, but now if they didn't get run over he was safe—limping noticeably with Liberati's help toward the first-aid center in the middle of the track. Richard Petty was already there. Like Bodine, he was out of the race and he hurried to check on the condition of his son. Felix Sabates was right behind. He seemed different now—his expression softer and his anger gone, as if the wreck had put things in perspective.

Ernie Irvan was also there, and he put his arm around Kyle and looked at him hard.

"Man," he said, "are you all right?"

On the fringes of the scene, Robin shook his head and tried to smile. It had been a bad day. They had finished 18th and lost a car, but their driver was alive and from all indications he was not badly hurt—maybe a bruise on his bad left leg. It was eerie to think that they were going next week to Talladega, where Petty had been injured the year before. But Robin tried not to think about it now; he just had to hope they would be all right.

PART TWO

PROGRESS

CHAPTER 5

FROM TALLADEGA TO THE ALL-STAR BREAK

It was a strange weekend in Talladega. Something about the setting was unreal. Here they were in an all-white enclave, with Confederate flags snapping in the infield breeze, and everywhere around the country was burning down. This was the week of the Rodney King verdict. A jury with no blacks in southern California had acquitted four white policemen of beating King, a black man, even though the beating had been videotaped. Riots erupted, and by race day Sunday, forty-six people were dead in Los Angeles. Outbursts of violence had spread to Atlanta, New York, even Birmingham a few miles away, and Kyle Petty was struck by the irony of it.

He remembered pieces of history he had read—particularly a scene from 1961, when the Freedom Riders' bus was burned in Anniston. It was Mother's Day, May 14, when a mob attacked the Greyhound bus, which carried black and white passengers traveling together. They slashed the tires and smashed the windows, and when the tires went flat a few miles up the road, the mob struck again—this time setting the bus on fire. Kyle Petty knew the story in detail. He had become an avid reader of history, and there was something about the whole civil rights epic—young activists willing to risk their lives and the ugliness they revealed in the world as it was. The events in Anniston seemed especially ironic, for they had happened very close to where the track now stood. Petty thought conditions had changed since then. People in the South seemed less hung up, and black fans certainly were accepted at the races. Still the divisions persisted across the country, and their own sport of racing was a testament to it. All you had to do was look around. Only one black driver, Wendell Scott, had ever won a race at the Winston Cup level, and the crowds every week were 90 percent white.

In Talladega, all of those thoughts came and went in Petty's mind, particularly at night when he turned on the television back in his room, but they never quite made it to center stage, for there were other realities that were simply too pressing. This was his first return to Talladega—his first competition at the fastest track in NASCAR since his terrible wreck from the year before. He still had a metal rod in his leg, holding the once-jagged pieces of his femur together, allowing them to mend. Of course he still remembered the pain and the sound of his screams that chilled even the medics who pulled him from the car. For days he lay in the hospital bed, reality a blur, with the fever and infection racing through his body, and Pattie at his side.

After a few days, the suffering gave way to hours of idle time when all he could do was read and think. Books had been his passion for years—not so much as a child when he resented the meddling of his teachers in school and was bored with nearly everything they assigned. His fifth-grade teacher had a different idea. "Let him read anything he wants," Sarah Toomes told his mother, Lynda. *Hot Rod, Motor Trend, Popular Mechanics*—it didn't really matter, as long as a boy developed good habits. Later, when Kyle graduated from high school, he began to think about the things he had missed—all those times he had just coasted through, reading the Cliff Notes instead of Shakespeare. He had given up college for a career on the tracks, but that didn't mean he had to be ignorant. He plunged into the task of reading good books. He read Hemingway, Faulkner and Solzhenitsyn, as well as a few writers from closer to home—Clyde Edgerton, Kaye Gibbons and Dori Sanders.

After his wreck he read *The Grapes of Wrath*, and it hit him hard on several different levels. He was caught up in the eloquence of Steinbeck's prose and the story of a family that had lost everything. It reminded him of things his grandparents told him—memories of life in the Great Depression. There was more as well. "It was the story of people wanting to do right, wanting to get ahead," he remembers. But there always seemed to be something in the way—some set of forces that they couldn't control.

Petty could identify with the theme, for more and more as the days went by, he was thinking about his difficult recovery—and how much he hated not being in a car. The idea was almost irrational at first. Here he was, battered by a wreck that could easily have killed him, and he was counting the days until he could risk it again. There was something about this crazy career, something in his blood, and his ordeal had brought it all into focus. Racing gave him that feeling of purpose, and the funny thing was, it was the only thing in his life that ever came hard.

"Kyle was always Mr. Perfect," says his sister, Sharon, who had to follow behind him in school. "Everybody loved him—all the girls, all the guys, all the teachers. Everything he wanted to do was easy. He could play tennis like a pro the first time he tried. He could get up and ski the first time out, or play a guitar the first time he picked it up. He always had that magic touch."

Dale Inman, Richard Petty's cousin and long-time crew chief, has the same memory of Kyle as a boy. Whether it was playing football or welding the pieces together on a car, somehow Kyle could make it look easy. Even racing was that way at first. Inman remembers the first time out—Daytona 1979. Kyle was eighteen and already pestering his father to let him drive. They had some Chrysler cars out back—pretty good pieces of equipment overall that they no longer used because Chrysler was starting to pull out of the sport. They decided to take an old Dodge to Daytona and let Kyle drive it in the ARCA race. Inman remembers they were all pretty nervous, with Richard Petty the most nervous of all. "Just be careful," he told his son. "Win, lose, or draw, it doesn't matter to me."

Kyle was careful, and he also won. He drove his car to the outside pole, and was in and out of the lead all day. He took over for good with seven laps to go, and held off the pole-sitter, John Rezak. Like everybody else, Dale Inman was astonished. "He had hardly driven a race car down the driveway," he said. That was Kyle. For the teenaged son of Richard Petty, nothing in the world seemed to be very hard.

Soon, however, that perception disappeared, for Kyle began racing on the Winston Cup circuit—five times in 1979, fifteen the next year and a full schedule in '81. Now he was running with the best in the world, and it took him seven years to win at that level. After a while a lot of fans, and even a few people around the garage, began to whisper that he was a genetic aberration—a Petty with no talent for driving a race car. Dale Inman had a different analysis. In a sport as competitive as racing, he said, it's hard to move from the top 20 to the top 5, and talent is only one ingredient in the change. The bigger question was just as basic: whether Kyle really had the focus and desire.

For a while, there was reason to believe he didn't. He indulged his interest in other things—read a lot of books and wrote stories for his children and even played around with a career in country music. He sang on the stage of the Grand Ole Opry, and worked on an album for RCA, and some people said that was really his love. In 1990 everything changed. At Rockingham in the spring, he won the biggest purse in the history of NASCAR, and his dreams grew quickly in proportion after that. At the age of thirty, Kyle began to talk about a championship season—about carving his niche in the history of the sport—and his resolve grew deeper with the wreck in Talladega. He knew as he lay in his hospital bed, or in the weeks after that as he began his convalescence, that he was doing precisely what he wanted to do, and his only goal now was to try to do it better. In May of 1992, when they returned once again to the Talladega Speedway, Robin Pemberton could see it in his eyes.

What he didn't see was fear, though he knew it had to be there somewhere. "It would be for me," Robin said before the race. They did what they could to combat it systematically—with 1,800 miles of testing—but there was still something about the second turn, where Petty had crashed with Ernie Irvan, and something about a track where drivers rarely put on the brakes. There was a time at Talladega in the 1980s when 200 m.p.h. was slow. But after a few spectacular crashes—cars leaving the track, traveling at the takeoff speeds of a jet—the insurance companies began having nightmares: What if a car made it into the stands? NASCAR moved to change the rules, requiring cars at Talladega and Daytona, the two fastest tracks, to use restrictor plates—square pieces of metal with four small holes, each ⅞ of an inch in diameter—to reduce the flow of air to the manifold. The effect was to cut horsepower by a third.

Most drivers didn't like the arrangement very much. They thought it carried its own set of problems. What you got at Talladega was a long train of cars running single file, since that way they punched a bigger hole in the air and could draft together at much higher speeds. The restrictor plates cut their power so much that it was hard to break out of line to pass. The result was sometimes boring for fans, lap after lap with little change in the field—and when drivers did see an opening, even the smallest chance to make a move, as Ernie Irvan did before his wreck with Petty, they often felt obliged to take it.

The worst part was, even with restrictors, cars occasionally took flight and wrecked in the most spectacular fashion. But those were the rules at Talladega, and the drivers did their best to adjust.

In May of 1992, Petty was working hard at it in practice, trying to recapture his Talladega rhythm, and trying to block the distractions from his mind. It was not easy. In addition to the nagging question of fear, which reporters seemed intent on bringing to his attention, the rumor mill was in full swing. It happened every year about this time, so predictable and so absurd that people in racing had a name for it—"Silly season,"—a time when press agents scrambled to head off stories and owners and drivers had to huff their denials. The premise of the whole exercise was simple. By now the season was assuming a shape: Some teams were running well and some were not, and those that were mired in the latter category were all assumed to be making changes. Petty's team was no ex-

ception. That weekend in his hometown paper, there was a report—
a "hot rumor," the sports editor called it—that Sabates had made
an offer to Dale Earnhardt, apparently to replace Petty in 1994.

Even though Sabates immediately denied it, Petty hated to see
it in print. It was one more distraction for the guys on the team,
just when things seemed to be getting better. Felix had met with
the whole group Monday—the day after his Martinsville tirade
when he had complained about the season to anyone who would
listen. On Monday he told them they were doing a good job, and
that success would come if they just kept at it. Kyle was glad to
hear him say it—for Robin's sake, as much as anyone's. In the first
three months of their difficult season, Robin had made a lot of
changes in the car: the springs, the shocks, the gears, the motor—
the setups were different from Gary Nelson's, and there had been
no success to prove him right. Kyle knew his crew chief could use
the vote of confidence.

Now, however, there was the rumor about Earnhardt, and Petty
was worried about another blow to morale. His wife, Pattie, was
furious about it. "Nobody works good under a cloud," she told
one reporter, and she blamed the whole problem on Sabates; he
had been so vocal in Martinsville that he simply invited this kind of
speculation. Pattie was ferocious in defense of her husband, and
some of his team members grumbled about it. They said she was
only making it worse, adding a new layer of controversy and distraction.

All in all, Kyle was grateful when the race finally started.

It was a warm day at the track, with the heat waves shimmering
toward the Appalachian Mountains while a bank of thunderclouds
hovered to the west. The crowd was huge, and Petty was nervous—
but no more so than Felix Sabates, who had been badly frightened
the week before when he saw his driver in a burning car. It was the
ugly and frightening side of racing—a level of danger that made
you wonder sometimes if the sport was worth it. Felix had his own
memories of the wreck at Talladega, waiting in the infield first-aid
center while the rescue workers cut the roof off the car. The tension
mounted as the minutes ticked away. Pattie was there, and Kyle's
mother, Lynda, and Richard Petty, who was out of the race. They

were relieved momentarily when Dale Jarrett came in, reporting simply that Kyle had hurt his leg. Jarrett, too, had been caught in the wreck, and when he got out of his car, he heard Petty's screams and ran over and crawled through the passenger window. "Be still," he told him, and he waited with him until the rescue began. When Jarrett made it to the first-aid center, he didn't tell the Pettys how bad it looked—how there was a piece of bone that had sliced through the skin, and how Kyle had been afraid that his leg was severed. But Sabates and the others soon knew it was bad, and the memories were strong when they came back to Talladega. "This is a race we want over and done with," Felix told one reporter. "For us in a way, the season starts after this one."

Thus it was tense in the pits when they got the green flag, and even more so as Petty began losing ground. After starting 9th, he lost ten positions in the first three laps, and after six laps he was 32nd. But then he seemed to get his rhythm, drafting with Greg Sacks and Bobby Hillin, and all of a sudden he was as fast as the leaders—a dizzying pace, at 196 m.p.h.

"Just relax," said Robin Pemberton, his voice reassuring and matter-of-fact. "Pick your way back through it. You're doing real good."

By lap 16, he had worked his way to 24th and was now in a draft with Buddy Baker, the legendary giant of a race car driver who was looking for his 20th Winston Cup win, but at age fifty had recently cut back to a limited schedule. Baker could still drive, and he and Kyle and Michael Waltrip were now in line in a three-car draft—as fast as anybody on the track. "You're doing good," Robin told him again. "Keep digging." By lap 24 he was passing good cars—Dale Jarrett, Hut Stricklin, and Bobby Hamilton—and by lap 44 he was in the top 10. Then, once again, he ran into problems.

He pitted for two tires on lap 48, and they made an adjustment to tighten the chassis. It was a good stop—Kyle came in 10th and went out 7th, but when he returned to the track, he found himself running his laps alone. There weren't any cars close enough to draft with, which meant he was slow, and for an agonizing period of nearly ten laps he lost ground steadily on the cars he was chasing. Robin's voice on the radio was cool.

"Here comes your buddy," he said, referring to Ernie Irvan who was gaining from behind. "Hook up with him. You're gonna catch those guys in front."

They did hook up with Kyle in the lead, and immediately their speeds began to soar. They were gaining visibly on the cars ahead, when Ernie did a peculiar thing. He pulled out to pass, which broke the draft and slowed both cars. "He thinks he's faster," said Steve Knipe, the spotter. Kyle muttered something on the radio, and fell in behind. At the moment, of course, it didn't really matter who was in front, so long as they found the fastest combination. The idea was to catch the lead draft of cars; once they did that it was every man for himself.

After a few laps, the verdict was clear: They were a full second faster with Petty in the lead. It was hard to understand the reason for that—some peculiarity of aerodynamics—but Robin rushed down to Ernie's pit and explained the situation to his chief, Tony Glover. Glover, a reasonable man, agreed, and radioed Ernie to fall in behind. To everyone's amazement, Irvan refused.

A year or two earlier it would have been no surprise. Ernie was a legend for his recklessly bad judgment—an impatience that put him into dicey situations and sometimes caused major problems on the track. As often as not, he was a victim of his own mistakes— wrecking sometimes with a dozen other cars, all because he lacked the patience to wait. But in 1992, he was different. Ever since Daytona, when he was blamed for a wreck that destroyed the best cars, and certainly since Atlanta, when he broke his collarbone, people said Ernie was using better judgment. Kyle had noticed and was proud of him for it. He was convinced that Ernie would soon be a star: He had superb ability as a driver—competitive and tough, a nice guy off the track. The only missing piece was a little more patience, and Ernie himself was beginning to see it. "Patience," he told one reporter that week, "is the hardest thing to learn and the easiest to forget—and when you do, it jumps out and bites you."

Now once again, Irvan's competitiveness was interfering with his judgment, and Petty was mystified. With Kyle in front, they were catching other cars. With Ernie in front they were not. But Ernie insisted on being in front.

"Is this four-car dumb, or what?" said Petty, referring to the number on Irvan's door.

Robin, in the pits, shook his head in disbelief. "He's the dumbest sumbitch I've ever seen."

To be fair, that was racing in Talladega. Crew chiefs scrambled to make little deals, trying to decide which teams could help them and which ones couldn't; drivers were racing around the track at a blur, and everyone was making split-second decisions. All in all, it was a nerve-wracking business, and almost everybody made their mistakes. One of Kyle's came at the halfway point. He was battling Ricky Rudd for 7th position, and he ducked low to pass on the inside groove. There was a string of cars in the draft behind them, and Kyle was sure that somebody would follow, creating a second draft for speed. Unfortunately, nobody came, which meant he was hung out by himself—his car suddenly slower than those in the line. He fell all the way to 14th position, and his voice on the radio was depressed.

"I don't know what I was thinking," he said.

That's the way it went for the rest of the race—ebbs and flows and mounting frustration—and with less than twenty laps to go, Petty let it show in a way that he regretted. Never once in their difficult season had he ever criticized a member of the crew—not in Darlington when the engine burned up, not in Rockingham when he was supposed to win and the car was so bad it made him look awful. His reasons for that were simple enough. There was nothing worse for a team than dissension, nothing harder on morale than a condescending driver. Besides, he knew that the guys were working hard. They had built great cars for the short track races, and he had wrecked every time. He was beginning to feel he had let them down, and the last thing he wanted was to seem ungrateful.

Despite this, with eighteen laps to go in Talladega, he slipped. He was in a large group of cars with no order to it—some passing high, some trying low and some willing to go three abreast in the turns. He needed help from his spotter, Steve Knipe, but Knipe was having a difficult time. For people trying to do his job, the Talladega track is probably the worst. At most places, the roof where they sit is high enough to see the whole field. At Talladega, it isn't, and the track is so huge—2.66 miles around—that even when Knipe had a clear line of vision, the cars in some places looked like ants. Several times during the afternoon, other cars passed Petty before Knipe could warn him—and now in the waning stages of the race, they were losing precious ground as Irvan and Kulwicki got by low, and Petty was trapped behind Derrike Cope.

"Steve," he said, "you ain't helping much right now."

There was a split second of silence before Petty caught himself. He liked Steve Knipe—a quick-witted man, quiet and conscientious, the kind of person who did his best and would probably take the criticism to heart. Petty knew all that, and even in traffic at 195 m.p.h., it dawned on him clearly that he had made a mistake. When he spoke again, his voice was soft and he tried to make amends. "That's okay, man," he said.

The radio fell silent after that, and the race seemed headed for an unhappy ending. Kyle had been in and out of the top 10 all day, but with less than fifteen laps to go he had faded all the way to 16th. He wanted to salvage something better than that, but everybody was racing hard right now. There were twenty cars battling for the top 10 positions, and Kyle was in the middle of a pack of eighteen. On the backstretch with less than twelve laps to go, he tried to squeeze between the wall and Wally Dallenbach. There wasn't enough room, and the two cars bumped, which immediately set off a chain reaction. Dallenbach lurched to the left and bumped Jimmy Spencer, whose car began to spin and then took off. The wind got beneath it on the infield grass, and it became a missile— soaring end-first for a thousand feet, with only the nose of the hood touching ground. It was one of those breathtaking moments of terror, disaster waiting at the end of the flight. The car was sideways when it finally hit the ground, which meant it should have flipped and rolled like a barrel. Instead, it bounced and came down neatly on all four tires with the front end pointed straight up the track. To everybody's relief, Spencer was fine.

After the race, Petty acknowledged that the wreck was his fault, but at the moment he had to put it out of his mind. There were nine laps to go when they restarted the race, and Petty was still in 13th position. With so little time, and so many cars bunched together at the front, it was plain to see it wouldn't get any easier. He maneuvered quickly into a battle for 10th, but Mark Martin was there, along with Rusty Wallace and Alan Kulwicki, and the racing by now was almost frantic. With three laps to go, Petty was high on the track coming into turn 2, exactly where he'd wrecked the year before, and he saw an opening to go three abreast. There was no time now to think about the past—about his crash with Ernie and the slow-motion spin and the sickening blur of pain in his leg. There was only the split-second chance to move, and Petty took it. He dove low down the track beneath Rusty Wallace, and his momentum put him in 10th position. He held onto it for three more laps.

"Good job, guys," he said when he finished.

Back at the truck, as they were loading the car, Felix came by to pronounce a benediction. Finally, he said, they had scrapped their way to a top 10 finish, and Kyle and the car were both in one piece. All in all, it was not a bad day.

Robin agreed, but he hoped for better a couple of weeks down the road when they made a two-race stop in Charlotte. Those were both high-dollar events, beginning with an all-star race, The Winston, and Robin had a special reason to be excited. In the last few weeks, they had built a new car, and he said he felt like a football coach who was finally able to work with his own recruits. They had made a lot of changes in Gary Nelson's cars, but Robin still wasn't satisfied with them. He was looking forward to running with something all his own.

Jane Gossage was excited also. As the public relations representative for Petty and his corporate sponsor, Mello Yello, she had lived through the ups and downs of the season, and she had a premonition that it was all going to change. Part of it was simply her knowledge of the sport; she thought she could see some improvement every week. Yet there was something else playing around in her mind, even though it sounded a little funny to admit it. A few days earlier, almost as a joke, they had asked a psychic from over in the mountains how Kyle would fare during the rest of the season. The psychic said he would win two races.

And what about the all-star race coming up?

Kyle at 200 m.p.h.

The psychic said he would come in second.

Jane knew better than to bet the house on it, but on the other hand, it had been a tough year. For the moment at least, she was willing to believe.

CHAPTER 6

RUNNING WITH THE BEST

There was a funny new mood in Charlotte this time, a mixture of excitement and low-grade fear. They had decided to run The Winston at night, and some people said it couldn't be done. There was simply no way to light a track that huge, exactly a mile and a half in circumference, without a combination of shadows and glare. The drivers were convinced it would be unsafe, and Dale Earnhardt was the most outspoken. He said it was crazy.

Kyle Petty thought Earnhardt was right. But he also knew that if they could do it anywhere they could do it in Charlotte, where the speedway president, Humpy Wheeler, had pulled off a few crazy things in his life. As a kid, Wheeler fought in the streets of Belmont, a little mill town just west of the city, and later, he became a Golden Gloves boxer and raced an old Packard on the red clay tracks and played football at South Carolina. Then he broke his back on the football field, and sports gave way to the world of the mind. Wheeler became a racing promoter, a kind of P. T. Barnum of the Southern dirt tracks, working his way through the levels of the sport. He signed on at Charlotte in 1975, and it was a low-rent facility back in those days. The grandstand was old and the bathrooms were dirty; it fit in perfectly with the image of the sport. Yet Humpy had a different image in his head. There were times when he'd stare from the window of his office, across the dull blue horizon of the Piedmont Hills, and he would imagine where racing could be in ten years. It wasn't that he wanted to alter it a lot. Even today, his eyes light up as he tells the old stories—drivers power-sliding into the turns and showers of clay raining down on the fans. There was something elemental about the competition, a hillbilly throwback to the days of the chariot, and Wheeler didn't want to lose that feeling. He just believed it was possible to improve on the setting.

At Charlotte, that's what he set out to do, and he and the owner, Bruton Smith, plowed their profits back into the track. They built a new grandstand and better bathrooms, followed later by glass suites and luxury condominiums. After a while, they began to see a difference. The first thing they noticed was that women were starting to show up at the track—not just a few in tight-fitting jeans, but wives with husbands and mothers with children, and some from a whole different corner of society. Some people believed, as late as the seventies, that racing was essentially a working-class sport. Somehow it fit with the blue-collar life—this crazy competition where the shining moment was always out there, but most of the time you came up short. The guy in the stands could understand that. You worked and struggled, and bad luck came and bit you in the ass.

Wheeler didn't want to turn away from those people—they were loyal fans and the pillars of the sport, but he could see already where the growth market was: women and families and the white-collar crowd. Humpy felt sure he could reach them all. The competition on the track was only getting better with the infusion of money from the corporate sponsors, but racing had an image problem to overcome, much like the NFL in the 1950s, or the NBA even later than that. In a way, it was the opposite image from golf, which was viewed by many as a country-club sport, an elitist pastime that was essentially inaccessible. Racing was accessible, no doubt about that, but too many people stayed away on purpose.

Wheeler could see that beginning to change, as he and Bruton Smith continued their improvements—more condominiums, a glass office tower and a $20 million Speedway Club where the food was prepared by a European chef. Critics scoffed at the sport's new pretensions, but Wheeler merely shrugged. He was certain that the critics were wrong. His mission, as he saw it, was not to change the basic character of racing, but to add something to it—to make a rich tradition even richer—and of all the things they had done in Charlotte, nothing was more important to that goal than the lights.

He remembered the night when he was playing football, and the team made a trip down to LSU. It was a madhouse—a packed grandstand in voodoo country, with a tiger pacing near the other team's bench, and people going crazy, and somehow at night everything was more intense. The colors were vivid. The illusion of speed was almost startling—and he knew from experience that it was usually that way at a short track race. He wanted to create the same feeling in Charlotte—to add to the spectacle and boost ticket sales, and to give them a chance to race in prime time. More and more, the sport had developed a TV following—fans who rarely went to the track, but tuned in every week to ESPN, or wherever they could find a race on the cable. With the other weak offerings on Saturday night, a prime-time race was a chance for a breakthrough—but only, of course, if they could find a way to make it safe.

Their first try at it was nearly catastrophic. In December of 1991, the speedway staff put up some lights. They picked the first turn as a prototype because that was the fastest point on the track. If the lights worked there, they would work anywhere. They looked pretty good to Wheeler's eye, and Humpy volunteered to test them himself. He strapped himself in the pace car seat, crash helmet rumpling his wavy blond hair, and with his headlights on he took a few laps. On the third time around, he pushed his speed to 125 and cut his lights as he hit the first turn. The glare was so bad, he couldn't see a thing—couldn't even see the light switch on the dash. The only thing that saved him from wrecking the car was the fact that he had been around the track so often. "I think we better call in the experts," he said.

They called Musco, a company from Iowa with a strong resumé. It had done the Rose Bowl, among other arenas, but the speedway was nearly ten times as large, and there wasn't much time to figure it out. They could see right away that to avoid the combination of shadows and glare, the light had to come from both sides of the track. The trick was to do it without any poles—at least none that would obstruct the view of the fans. They decided to put lights on the grandstand roof, and on poles that circled the outside of the track. Inside, they installed a series of ground level lights that were aimed at mirrors, which in turn bounced the light to the asphalt surface. The plan was ingenious, which was reasonable to expect at a price of $1.7 million. But many of the drivers still had doubts and Kyle Petty was among them. It wasn't that he questioned the skill of engineers or their ability to solve the most obvious problems. "But speed is sight," he explained. When they raced at night the track would be a circular ribbon in the dark with everything blacked out beyond the edge. Petty was worried that that would be a problem. When they were running at places like Talladega, the tracks were huge and so was the drivers' field of vision. They could see a panorama of infield and sky, and somehow it muted their sense of speed—like pilots looking out from the window of a plane. Take that away, and Petty didn't know. Would it be too much for their reflexes to handle?

He was pleasantly surprised by the answer to his question. From the first practice session under the lights, on a cool Wednesday night with 38,000 people in the stands, nearly everyone agreed that the lighting was superb. Depth perception took some getting used to, but for Petty and the others, the adjustment came quickly. "Daytime at night," concluded Ken Schrader, and even Dale Earnhardt had to agree. "I've got no problem with these lights," he said. "There's no beginning or end. They decided to spend the money and do a night show right."

The real show began on May 15, some twenty-four hours before the Winston. This was qualifying night, and everybody was nervous. On Petty's team, they had their reasons. In a week of practice, their car had been fast, and it was long past time to have a good run. Talladega had been encouraging, but it was hard to forget their bump-and-grind run through the short track season, or the race at Darlington when the engine blew up. On each of those occasions they had been running well, and just when everybody started feeling good, started to *feel* the possibility of a win, something bad happened to snatch it away.

There was no use whining about the past: Always in racing, it was important to focus on the task just ahead, and on this particular night the task was strange. Instead of running a single lap to qualify, or maybe two, the way they did at most tracks, they had to run three and make a pit stop to change two tires. Pit stops were usually a time of pressure, and this time it was worse—no chance for redemption if the stop was bad.

Robin breathed deeply as they waited their turn, like a basketball player at the free throw line. It was almost time. Kyle was on the track, and his lap times were fast, and now he was roaring to a stop in the pit. Robin led the charge to the far side of the car, where he immediately began attacking the front lug nuts. His heart was pounding, as he loosened the nuts and pitched the old tire out of the way. Somehow, he could feel he was a little bit slow. He jammed the new tire in place and tightened the nuts, but Mike Ford was already dropping the jack, which was the prearranged signal for Petty to go. Robin jumped up and started his sprint back across the pit, but he managed to get tangled in the air wrench cord just as Petty hit the gas. For Kyle it was a moment of disbelief. His wheels were spinning as he stood on the throttle, and suddenly there was Robin right in front of him, stumbling on the cord as he tried to get free. Petty swerved to the right as best he could, but there wasn't even time to hit the brakes, as Robin made a dive for the pit road wall. Somehow he made it without being hit, but their pit stop was ruined, and their qualifying time was one of the worst. Petty would be starting the race 16th.

Robin's mood was grim for the next little while. He reassured Mike Ford, then quietly cursed his own ineptitude. "At least I didn't get killed," he muttered.

After a while, though, it began to seem funny. People were teasing him about his form, his slow motion-glide across the wall, which was airing that night on the TV sports. They were still laughing about it late Friday evening, as they climbed to the top of the transporter truck to get a better view of the Sportsman race. This one promised to be quite a show. Most of the Sportsmen were weekend drivers with virtually no experience on a superspeedway, which meant that they were likely to make some mistakes. Even worse, the field was crowded—nearly fifty cars racing for the last ten spots in the big Sportsmen race to be held the next night.

One of the drivers was Gary Batson, who ran a feed store in South Carolina. Batson was divorced, his parents were dead, and racing had become his weekend passion. He had been at it now for about seven years, mostly running short tracks over near Greenville. The Sportsman race was a new plateau, and he was doing pretty well when there was a spin just ahead coming out of turn 4. Batson swerved high to try to avoid it, squeezing toward the wall, when another driver, Neal Connell, tried to do the same thing. Connell and Batson ran together, and Batson's car flipped, sliding along with the driver's door down and the wheels against the wall. The cars spilled gas, which quickly caught fire in a shower of sparks. Connell was able to dive from his window, but Batson was trapped. The fire kept burning, and the people in the grandstand watched in horror, and still there was no sign of movement in the car. Finally, the rescue squad got there and cut Batson free, but he died the next day with burns over 80 percent of his body.

The drivers' garage was eerie after that. Geoff Bodine and one or two others were talking in hushed and stricken tones. Nobody expected anything like this, though in retrospect, you had to say it was an invitation to disaster: a track that was crowded with inexperienced drivers, most going faster than they ever had before. This was the ugly side of the sport—made even uglier by the official explanations. NASCAR vice-president Les Richter called the accident "most unfortunate," but said in effect that it couldn't be helped: Drivers had to get their experience somewhere. Richter was right about the catch-22. Experience was essential on a track like Charlotte's, and where could they get it except on the track?

For a brief time Friday, the garage was humming with that debate. it was the second death in three years at the Charlotte Speedway, and by anybody's standards the toll was too high. Several crew chiefs, standing in a huddle, blamed the crowded field—"too many cars on the track," they said, and it was easier to think about it that

THREE GENERATIONS OF NASCAR STARS:

Kyle.

The King.

Kyle's grandfather, Lee, the family's first champion.

An approaching storm in Darlington soon stops the race—making
Darrell Waltrip a winner.

The frontstretch in Daytona.

For Kyle, a pensive moment, waiting for practice.

The lights at the Charlotte Motor Speedway where Ernie Irvan takes a practice lap.

Kyle and his father racing side by side in Daytona.

Talking strategy in
Richard Petty's truck.

Kyle's car catches fire after a wreck in Martinsville.

Driver Geoff Bodine, already out of the race, rushes across the track to battle the blaze.

Tony Liberati of Wally Dallenbach's crew pulls Kyle from the car.

Kyle, his mother Lynda, and three sisters, Sharon, Lisa, and Rebecca, just before Richard Petty's last race.

Kyle's wife, Pattie, watches the start with mixed emotions.

Kyle in Victory Lane at
Watkins Glen.
(photo by Kevin Kane)

President Bush pays tribute to Richard Petty in Daytona.

A pit stop in Rockingham, where Kyle wins again.

Signing autographs at Indy.

way. If the flaw was essentially in the planning of the race, somehow that made their own drivers safer. Death still came in freakish forms. Once, years ago, Kyle had seen an uncle killed by an exploding air tank in Richard Petty's pit. The possibility was there, but at the level of the sport where the Pettys operated, you had to believe the chances were remote. The drivers were good and the cars were safe, and when race day came you didn't think about it. That's the way it was with the death of Gary Batson. The shock and the grief were there for a moment, and maybe they lingered somewhere beneath the surface, but on Saturday night it was time to move on. For the drivers, once again, it was time for the show.

There was a full moon rising at the Charlotte Speedway, a bright orange glow out across turn 3. Already, the lights were bouncing off the cars, and the grandstand was full and the crowd was buzzing. The format of the race was designed for high drama. There would be two segments of thirty laps each, with the field inverted at the end of the first—and then a ten-lap sprint to the end.

At stake was a purse of $800,000, with $50,000 to the winner of each segment, and $200,000 to the winner at the end. As always, the competitors were the best in the sport—former NASCAR champions and winners of races from the preceding year. Kyle was ready. They had gotten Talladega out of the way, and their Charlotte car was a killer in practice. Down in the pits, the crew sounded calm. "We'll try to give you a show," Robin told his owner, Felix Sabates, and then he said to Kyle, "Whether you win or come in 20th, we're behind you 100 percent."

There was a hint of real emotion in his voice, and Kyle picked it up. "Ten-four," he said. "You guys be careful."

When the green flag fell, the car was pretty good—maybe a little tight and pushy in the turns, but Petty was moving up. He passed Geoff Bodine and Harry Gant, and gained more ground when Dale Jarrett spun and wrecked four cars. Within a dozen laps Petty was ninth, but then his chassis began to stiffen, and the car was unresponsive in the turns. Mark Martin and Ernie Irvan both got by him, and Petty was 11th at the end of thirty laps. It was not a particularly impressive beginning, but they worked on the car during the break between heats, and put in a spring rubber—a hard, semi-circular piece of rubber that Robin likes to use to reduce the flexibility of the spring. When the car is too tight, the rubber goes on the right rear spring, and that part of the car tends to slide through the turns. With the rear end swinging in a looser arc, the car is easier to steer through the corners.

That, at least, is the way they draw it up, and in the second thirty-lap segment of The Winston, the difference was stunning. From the green flag on, Petty's Pontiac, which had been mediocre, was now the fastest thing on the track. He whipped through the traffic in only eight laps, passing his father and Dale Earnhardt, and then Geoff Bodine to take the lead. He hadn't led a lap since he started from the pole in Rockingham, but he was in a groove now, and gaining on the field. "Stay after it, man," said Robin from the pit. Petty did. For a dozen laps, he gained ground steadily on Dale Earnhardt and Ernie Irvan, and had a two-second lead with five laps to go. From the spotters tower, Steve Knipe was amazed. He had seldom seen Petty more completely in control—his rhythm perfect, his lap times the same every trip around. When the second heat ended, Petty was leading by a second and a half, and the Mello Yello Pontiac was still running strong—but everybody knew that this was The Winston, where anything could happen. Once in 1987, Elliot and Earnhardt were bumping and scraping all the way to the finish, and when Earnhardt won, Elliott rammed him on the cool-down lap. Two years later, Rusty Wallace was 2nd going into the last turn, and he hit Darrell Waltrip who was leading the race. Waltrip spun and Wallace won. "I hope he chokes on the money," Waltrip fumed at the end.

In 1992, Petty's plan was to avoid all that. He thought he had the car hold a good lead and stay out of trouble, and when the green flag fell for the final ten laps, that's how it appeared. After only one lap, Petty was leading by three car lengths, and he stretched it to six on the second time around. "Do it!" yelled Robin, but then there was trouble. Waltrip lost control and spun to the grass, which caused a caution that wiped out the lead. "I didn't need that," Petty mumbled to himself, but Robin told him to relax. "You can outrun the whole crowd," he said.

On the restart, they got away fast, but Petty and Earnhardt

scraped together and Petty had to battle to avoid a spin. Earnhardt and Davey Allison both got around him, but in less than a lap, Petty had recovered. He was closing in quickly on Allison's bumper, and with five laps to go he passed him for second. He was after Earnhardt now, and he had the best car.

They were nose to tail until the final lap, when Petty cut low coming out of turn 1 and tried to pass on the inside of the track. He made it as far as Earnhardt's door as they headed two abreast down the back straightaway. Earnhardt aimed left to block his path, driving Petty almost to the grass. Both of them were running at full speed now, about 180 m.p.h. as they headed toward the turn— at an angle both of them knew was wrong. They were too low on the track, and going too fast, and yet there was nothing else they could do. Whoever backed off was admitting defeat, and whoever didn't was likely to wreck.

They surged through the turn, with Petty pulling briefly into the lead, when suddenly, Earnhardt lost control, and his car went skidding in a cloud of smoke. For the first split second, it was hard to believe. Petty saw nothing but clear track ahead and the great Dale Earnhardt spinning away—in a slow-motion arc toward the concrete wall. Petty knew he had a chance to win, but almost as quickly he knew he had a problem. Davey Allison was coming in a hurry.

For the people in the stands it was something to see—Allison in his black-and-red Thunderbird Ford, a glittery blur in the full-moon night swooping low in the turn and hurtling toward the lead. They hit the front stretch door to door, with Petty on the outside standing on the gas. He had slowed momentarily when Earnhardt wrecked, trying to avoid getting caught in the spin. Allison had a better angle of vision. He could see his opening from a few lengths back—a chance to dive low and pass inside—and he didn't hesitate. His car scraped Petty's as Kyle tried to block him, driving him down to the edge of the grass—and there they were for the last quarter-mile, banging and scraping at 185 m.p.h., while the people in the grandstands were on their feet, their cheers ringing louder than the roar of the cars. This one was headed for a memorable finish, but for Petty the memories would be bittersweet. With a few feet to go, Allison pulled half a car length ahead, and as they crossed the finish line Petty hit the button on his radio mike and told his crew members staring from the pit: "My fault, guys."

Then, the radio was silent. Even the grandstand was suddenly quiet as a terrifying spectacle began to unfold. When Allison surged ahead of Petty at the finish, he also lost control of his car. Davey spun and hit the wall without slowing down, then spun again in a shower of sparks and slid to a stop on the edge of the grass. After that, he didn't move. His frightened crew members rushed to the scene, and found their driver unconscious in the seat. They could see he was breathing, but it was hard to tell how badly he was hurt as the rescue workers began to cut him from the car. A few minutes later he opened his eyes, and according to one account, he mumbled weakly, "Well, boys, what happened?"

They were pretty sure he'd be all right after that, but they flew him to the hospital to check for broken bones. Kyle watched the helicopter rising through the night, then searched through the crowd for Davey's wife, Liz. He told her he was sorry, and he felt a little better when she told him not to worry. Davey, she said, was going to be fine, and nobody thought Kyle had done it on purpose.

A few minutes later, alone with his thoughts, Petty tried to sort through the pieces of his mood. In a way, he knew he ought to feel good. He had just finished 2nd in an all-star race, pitting himself against the best in the world. In their High Noon battle in turns 3 and 4, it was Dale Earnhardt who didn't make it through. Petty could take some satisfaction in that, and he also had to feel good for the team. The guys had put a winning car on the track. The only problem was, the driver didn't win—and he kept replaying the ending in his mind. Should he have been more aggressive when Davey tried to pass him? Maybe just rammed him to the infield grass? Or had he been too aggressive as it was? Davey, after all, was carried away on a stretcher, and despite the simmering rivalry between them, it was also true that they were old friends. They had grown up together on the tracks of Dixie, playing football in the Talladega infield and splashing in the surf of Daytona Beach. Davey could be a complainer sometimes, blaming other people for his problems, and he had made himself such a clone of his father. Bobby liked to hunt, so did Davey. Bobby flew an airplane, so did

Davey. They walked, talked and acted just the same. If you liked one Allison, you were bound to like the other. Kyle and Richard Petty were not like that. Kyle knew his father looked at him sometimes and wondered at the curious workings of genetics. But if Kyle had tried to build a separate identity, and if it seemed sometimes that Davey had not, this was clearly not the time to feel superior. Davey, after all, had won the race.

As Petty sat alone in his transporter truck, running his fingers through his shoulder-length hair, those were the thoughts that were spinning in his head. There was one more: he was also thinking about Dale Earnhardt, who had smiled and high-fived him after the race, and told him he had done a hell of a job. Earnhardt could have been ugly about it, maybe claimed that Petty had wrecked him on purpose. Instead, he was unbelievably gracious, and Petty knew that he shouldn't have been surprised.

Dale's character was far more subtle than his image. People called him "The Intimidator," and there was a good bit of truth that went with the legend. As a driver, Earnhardt was bold and aggressive, and even between races he was fiercely competitive. Once in the fall of 1990, when Earnhardt and Mark Martin were battling for the title, the two of them were asked to pose for a picture. It was late in the season, and the tension was building and Earnhardt's mood was unpredictable. He never cared much for publicity gimmicks, and when the photographer asked him to take off his cap, he refused. The photographer smiled and tried to explain that since Mark Martin had come without a cap, the picture would look better if neither driver had one. Earnhardt glared and gestured toward Martin: "Let him get one." And Mark Martin did.

Kyle Petty laughed when he heard the story. It was petulant and silly, a mind game played against Earnhardt's rival. But the sport, in part, was psychological, and Dale did his best to cover all the angles. He was a complicated man, quiet and private, almost shy. He loved the solitary sports like hunting, the cool autumn days by himself in the woods, and away from the track he could be a good friend—generous and loyal toward people he liked. More than anything else, Earnhardt was a champion. Going into the season, he had won fifty-two races and five championships, and he was skillful and fearless and drove flat-out every second of the race. Now here he was at the end of The Winston, admitting in effect that Kyle had outdriven him.

"He's a hell of a racer," Earnhardt declared.

For Petty, it was all a little too much; he has a hard time when it comes to compliments. He is cocky and loose in his bearing at the track, laughing, teasing, telling funny stories. But most people close to him say it's an act—"a shell," says his mother, perhaps against a world that expected too much. Whatever the reason, it is Kyle Petty's habit to deflect every compliment that comes his way, sometimes with a joke, other times with a compliment for somebody else. With Dale Earnhardt, however, he just couldn't do it, and now he was alone in the transporter truck, staring at the floor with his head in his hands, as he replayed the evening again and again in his mind.

A reporter broke the silence to ask how he felt, and Petty couldn't answer. Everything was coming at him now in a rush—the near-miss finish, the wreck with Davey, the feeling once again that he had come up short. And there was also Earnhardt, the greatest driver in the sport, who had managed somehow to get behind his defenses. It was hard to overstate how much that meant, or to imagine who else could have had that effect. Maybe Richard Petty, but at the moment at least, he was nowhere around. So Kyle sat alone in the half-light of the truck, and tried to make sense out of everything he felt. Whatever his confusions and layers of doubt, he had to admit it had been quite a night.

A few days later, his mood was different. For one thing, Davey was out of the hospital. He called a press conference to say he was fine—just a concussion, bruised lung and some soreness in his ribs, not the kind of thing to keep him from a race.

Davey had a big one coming up the next week—the Coca-Cola 600 in Charlotte, the second high-stakes race in the city, with a million dollars waiting for him if he won. Davey was having a magnificent season. He had won the Daytona 500 and the Winston 500 in Talladega, the two biggest races of the year so far. Every season, a million dollar bonus was offered to any driver who could win three of the season's big four. Only Bill Elliott had ever collected, but Davey could do it if he won in Charlotte. "We'll be ready," he told the press. "I plan to drive all six-hundred miles."

The writers at the news conference nodded their approval, and then wanted to know how he felt about Petty. Some of them clearly expected fireworks, but Davey was gracious. "Kyle did what any other driver would have done," he said, "including myself. He tried to take as much track as he could. He called me Sunday and we talked about it. He was pretty shook up. He kept apologizing all over the place. I told him not to worry. I know he didn't do it on purpose."

Petty, meanwhile, told the reporters that he was pleased to see that Allison was okay, and then he set his mind to move on, for there was no use dwelling on The Winston anymore—the things that happened, or the things that might have with a little bit of luck. That race was over, and it was a pretty good stop. They had a strong car and came in second, and he could tell the morale on the team was high; they expected to do even better on Sunday. The Coca-Cola 600 was a grueling race, the longest of the year by a hundred miles, but Robin and the rest of the team couldn't wait. This was their chance to unveil a new car, a sleek Pontiac that Robin had designed, which was blowing everybody away in practice.

Building the car had been a labor of love. As always, the frame and roll bars had come ready-made, but the crew applied the sheet metal themselves, preserving the shape of a Pontiac Grand Prix, with a few subtle curves to improve the flow of air. Felix Sabates and the team's secretary, Kim Long, decided to name the car Ro- bino. Robin was embarrassed but went along with it. He was too delighted with the car to argue. It was faster than anything else in the shop, and in the practice rounds for the Coca-Cola 600, only Bill Elliott was able to keep up. There were a couple of others who were in there close, but with a little bit of luck, Robin thought they might win the pole.

Qualifying day was overcast and cool, at least in the morning. But the sun got hotter as the day wore on, and when the time finally came for the qualifying laps, everything depended on the shape of the clouds. They drifted in and out, high cumulus puffs that cooled the track as they floated overhead, then left it to broil as they drifted away. The drivers waited for their turn to run, glancing uneasily from time to time at the heavens, hoping that the gods were on their side. Some, like Ricky Rudd, were lucky. A big cloud came, and the track got cool, and he ran a fast lap—30.814 seconds, a speed of 175.245. Bill Elliott, too, caught the edge of a cloud, and he was even faster at 30.773. But when Kyle's turn came after fourteen other drivers had run, the clouds blew away and the sun beat down on the sticky asphalt. Still, he knew that the car was fast, and he stood on the gas and hoped for the best. He liked this track, with nicely banked turns of 25 degrees, and he could tell as he drove it that his lap was a good one—not good enough to beat Bill Elliott, but fast enough for second and the outside pole.

Petty didn't want to talk about it much—"Sometimes we're fast, sometimes we're not," he said—but Robin smiled and knew they were ready.

When race day came, it was unbelievably hot—easily the hottest day of the year, and this was bad news. The race was brutal enough as it was—six hundred miles, like driving from Charlotte to Daytona with the windows rolled up and a winter coat on. The guys on the crew were still in a good mood, feeling as confident as they had all year. "All we need today is lady luck," said Richard Bostic, the driver of the truck.

Out in the car, Petty seemed tense, snappish, complaining about his radio connection to the pit. "These radios are shit," he said. The tension broke when the race finally started, and Kyle was immediately in a battle for the lead. Elliott, on the pole, got off slowly, and Petty and Ricky Rudd both made it around him—Rudd diving low to lead the first lap. For awhile, it appeared that Rudd would pull away, but Kyle held on and cut the lead, and by lap number 8 he was in first place. The car, however, was not quite right. "It's a little loose going into the corner," said Petty. "We need to put some more spoiler on it."

Robin was not surprised to hear it. The spoiler—that strip of metal running across the rear deck—was a crucial ingredient on a track like Charlotte, where a car's rear end could get loose in a hurry. The steeper the angle between the spoiler and the deck, the more it caught the air rushing past, creating a downforce that held the car steady. It was a delicate balance. Too much spoiler could slow you down, too little could cause you to slip and slide—and you never really knew until the race was underway. "Ten-four," said Robin. "We'll fix it as soon as we get a chance to pit."

The chance arrived on the 14th lap, when Richard Petty wrecked coming out of turn 4, spinning to a stop in the middle of the track. Kyle rushed in for four new tires and a spoiler adjustment, but most of the other cars didn't pit. When the race restarted, Kyle was 28th. There was nothing to do now except pick his way through the field, and for the next fifty laps that's what he did— passing the mediocre cars of Harry Gant and Dave Mader, and eventually the fast ones of Bill Elliott, Rusty Wallace, and Terry Labonte. On lap 66, he passed Mark Martin, and once again he was in 1st place.

By now it was clear that the car was fast, but Robin was worried about whether it would last. They were running a new cylinder head this time—state of the art from General Motors—which was supposed to add horsepower to the engine. To Robin's eye, it looked pretty fragile, but John Wilson thought they should give it a try. "If it works, it works," he said. "We might as well find out." It was hard to argue with that kind of logic, and Robin knew at this point in the year, there was nothing to be gained by being too timid. They had fallen way behind in the season's point standings, and if they were going to catch up they had to take risks. So far, so good in the Coca-Cola 600.

There was a scary moment on lap 111, when somebody blew an engine and left oil on the track, and Kyle ran through it before any of the race officials knew it was there. "I just about busted my ass," he reported. Thirty laps later there were still more hazards— a crash in turn 1, with Petty barely squeezing through the swirl of cars, and an even bigger wreck when the race restarted. Steve Knipe saw it before Petty did. "Back it down," he yelled. "Cars are crashing all over the place." Petty did, but several cars started wrecking behind him, and Petty was rammed by a spinning Dale Jarrett. It was beginning to feel like a short-track race.

The damage to the car was minor, however, and after the caution Petty began to pick his way through the field, moving from ninth to fourth in the next fifty laps, and then passing Davey Allison for third. Harry Gant was next and Kyle caught him quickly, then set his sights on Alan Kulwicki. After a few laps, they were two abreast—six inches apart at 175 m.p.h., while the crowd in the grandstand roared its approval. There were 160,000 people at the race, bringing the two-week total in Charlotte to 400,000. This was the heart of racing country, the epicenter of the sport, with most of the teams and a million fans nearby—and it was clear by now that nobody was leaving the city shortchanged. The boys on the track were putting on a show, and the star for the next hundred laps was Petty. He passed Kulwicki, and after twenty laps was ten lengths ahead of the next fastest car. Every now and then there were wrecks, producing cautions that took away his lead, but never for long. By lap 280, he was fifteen lengths ahead of Ernie Irvan, who had moved into second.

The car had been loose a little earlier in the day, but now it seemed to be running just right, and as they approached the 500th mile of the race, Petty was two seconds ahead of the field. It was hard to believe they still had another hundred miles to go—probably the toughest hundred miles in the sport—but he was feeling good as they made their last pit stop for tires. They were hanging on to the lead over Ernie, and Dale Earnhardt, who was now running 3rd, was nearly three seconds back. Their pit stop was great—less than twenty seconds—but when Petty roared off to return to the track, he was astonished to discover he was in 3rd place. Irvan was 2nd; his team had had an even better stop. Incredibly enough, Earnhardt was first—and Petty didn't see how that was possible. Nobody changed four tires in sixteen seconds, which is what the Earnhardt crew would have had to have done to make up a three-second gap on the track. Something was fishy about the whole thing, but there was no time to worry about it now. He had a race to finish and two cars to catch, and on lap 349 he passed Ernie Irvan.

Even then, however, he could tell that something about the car wasn't right. The track had changed, and he could feel his Pontiac pushing in the corners. They needed a caution to make an adjustment, but they just couldn't get it. There had been so many of them early in the race, but now the laps continued to tick away, mile after mile, and the car got worse.

Ernie Irvan passed him on lap 360, and Petty watched helplessly as Ernie drove away in pursuit of Earnhardt. The finish was exciting—Ernie bearing down on Earnhardt's bumper, but never quite able to get around him, while Kyle crossed the line a distant third.

When the race was over he climbed from the car and stalked away quickly to the transporter truck, refusing live interviews with the TV people. Felix Sabates tried to console him. He had already told the whole team he was proud, and he said the same thing to Petty, his arm around his shoulder. This was the Sabates that most people knew. He was capable of anger at the guys on his team; he had shown that at Martinsville, when they qualified 17th after a series of mediocre finishes. But most of the time that was not his way; he was warm by nature and full of kind words, and had an instinct for being a leader. He could see that Kyle was bitterly disappointed—he had led more laps than any other driver, but for the second straight race he had finished just short. Sabates tried to make him feel better. "You drove a hell of a race," he said. "We're very proud."

Petty nodded and tried to respond. He appreciated what Sabates was doing—the class it took to shove aside his own disappointment and try to take care of the feelings of the team. It was the kind of thing a lot of owners didn't do, and yet in a way it missed the point. It was true that Kyle was upset by his finish, but even more than that he was mad at Earnhardt—and madder still at the NASCAR officials who let him get away with breaking the rules. Dale had gained at least three seconds on his last pit stop, and Kyle was certain that the only way he did it was by ignoring the speed limit on pit road. Nobody else got away with that, and Petty was frustrated—as much for Ernie Irvan as himself.

"Ernie's car outran me at the end," he told reporters. He had taken a few minutes to compose himself, and now he could choose his words with care. "Ernie," he said, "should have won the race."

And yet, it was also true that the Coca-Cola 600 was over, and as his father had taught him, you had to let it go. He began to wander among the members of his crew, forcing himself to tell funny stories, when he saw his wife on the edge of the crowd.

"Hey, what do you think?" he called out to her.

Pattie Petty tried to smile, but it never quite formed, and instead she answered his question with a shrug.

She was never very good at concealing her emotions—and somehow it was an appropriate summation of the day.

CHAPTER 7

COAST TO COAST

The next weekend, the tour moved north to Dover, Delaware. For Kyle and the crew, the disappointment of not winning faded quickly after Charlotte. What endured in its place was a feeling that they might be turning a corner. "Things have begun to change," Petty told one reporter. "From May of 1991, when we had our wreck in Talladega, until May of this year, it was one solid year of ungodly bad luck."

The last few weeks had been a lot better, with two top fives and a tenth in Talladega, and the morale on the team was visibly improved. They were smiling more and moving with confidence as they worked on the car, and nobody was happier than Big John Youk. Youk is a mechanic from Pennsylvania, the only part-timer on the Kyle Petty crew. He comes to every race on the northern end of the circuit—from Dover to Watkins Glen—doing whatever he can to help. He works for the price of his motel room, and maybe the cost of a meal here and there, but he doesn't mind. There are two main passions that define his life. The first is hunting deer in the Pocono woods, where he loves the quiet of the cool autumn mornings. He can sit for hours at the base of a tree, watching the leaves flutter down from overhead. Some fall quickly, while others are shaped like the wings of a bird and seem to take forever as they drift with the wind. Big John likes to study such things, for there is something sacred about the stillness of the woods—something very different from the NASCAR garage, which is loud and unruly with carbon monoxide fumes everywhere, and the race engines whining like a swarm of angry bees. Yet there's something about that too—the comraderie and competition and the adrenaline rush of being in the pits. It's true that you have to be a maniac to love it, jumping over the wall with cars whizzing by, trying to change a set of tires in nineteen seconds, but Big John admits that he meets that description. "It gets in your blood," he explains with a smile—especially on days when things are going well.

For the Mello Yello team, that's the way it was on the first day in Dover. It was a beautiful morning, with temperatures in the seventies and barely a cloud in the pale blue sky. Out on the speedway—the Monster Mile, as the writers like to call it—most of Petty's laps were smooth and efficient, while other good cars kept hitting the wall.

Some people said it was the radial tires. Goodyear had introduced them at Dover this time. It was part of a phase-out of the old bias plys, which were essentially four layers of rubber-coated plastic that tended to expand during the heat of a race. The circumference of tires was a tricky business anyway, with those on the right slightly bigger than the left, helping the car turn better in the corners. When the tires changed shape with the buildup of heat, it usually played havoc with the driver's control. Radial tires were not like that. They had a fiberglass belt between the layers of rubber, and when race teams inflated them with nitrogen gas, which was slower to respond as the tires got hot, the size never changed in the course of a race.

Most of the teams thought the radials were worth it, even at $984 a set. But any new tire took some getting used to, and for the first few hours of practice in Dover, a lot of good drivers were out of control. Harry Gant and Mark Martin each hit the wall, while Alan Kulwicki slammed into it twice.

Then the rains came. The bad weather rumbled on Friday night, and a cold, gray mist settled in across the state. There are few things grimmer than a rainy day at the track. With no way to practice, there's not a lot of work to be done on the cars, and after a while the teams are getting antsy. In Kyle Petty's truck, Dee Jetton and Ansle Hudson were sitting near the back, killing time. About mid-afternoon they began to reminisce. They are physical trainers for the Mello Yello crew, two attractive young women who run their own business. They call it Health Works, a combination of physical training and nutritional advice for individual clients and small corporate accounts. One of their earliest accounts was Chad Little, a Winston Cup driver who helped introduce them to the sport of racing. They were fascinated. Neither Jetton nor Hudson had ever thought much about the athletic demands on top race drivers—the elevated heart rate for three or four hours, the weight loss as high as ten pounds a race. In those ways, the drivers resembled long-distance runners—their bodies depleted by the long ordeal. The difference in the case of the NASCAR guys was that the demands on their reflexes did not diminish. In that way they were more like baseball players, who had to stay sharp as the game went on.

The funny thing was, a lot of good drivers were indifferent to conditioning. They ate junk food, and some of them partied too close to the race, and the guys on the pit crew could be even worse. Their jobs, too, were intensely physical, and required the most intricate small motor reflexes. Ansle Hudson thought the implications were staggering. What if a team got serious about training, working out every week and practicing their pit stops again and again? What kind of edge might they have over others? Hudson decided to take that notion to the top, and in the summer of 1991, she and Jetton went to see Richard Petty. They met him at the shop where he builds his cars, on a two-lane road that winds through the fields near the town of Level Cross, North Carolina. They found him cordial, as most people do, but he told them he thought his own time had passed. "I'm an old man," he explained with a smile. "I think you ought to talk to my son."

At ten the next morning, the telephone rang at the Health

Works office. It was Kyle Petty on the line. Dee Jetton, who took the call, expected somehow that it would be a hard sell, but Petty was responsive almost from the start. He had been through painful physical therapy, and he knew he still had a long way to go. He needed more strength in his wounded left leg, and a greater range of motion than he had after surgery. More than that, he needed the endurance for three-hour race, and he plunged wholeheartedly into the Health Works program. In all the hours spent lifting and stretching, hours when the pain was nearly overwhelming, Petty opened up to Hudson and Jetton. He talked about his job and how much it meant, about his crew and how the whole sport was the work of a team.

Both women were surprised by his subtle personality. He could seem so cocky and flippant on the surface, but beneath that exterior they found there was more. For one thing, Petty didn't seem bitter about his own bad luck, nor did he blame it on anybody else. In that way he seemed mature about life, able to accept the hard side of it—and yet he was also full of fun with a range of interests that left them amazed. Once in Phoenix, they were with him in the lounge of the transporter truck, and the TV was on in a corner overhead. Petty was laughing and flipping through the channels and offering a running commentary as he went. When they came to C-Span, he talked politics. When they came to the "National Geographic Explorer," featuring a documentary about Australia, he talked about the difference between kangaroos and wallabies and all of the oddities of evolution down under. But his favorite subject of the afternoon was Elvis. They came across the movie *Love Me Tender*, and Petty stopped flipping and watched for awhile. He said he knew he was the wrong age for it; by the time he began his teenage years, the king of rock 'n' roll was past his prime. Still, Petty was intrigued by Elvis Presley and all the ingredients that made up his success. Some of it was easy enough to understand. Presley had the talent to sing anything, from Delta blues to hard-core country, and he did it in a style that was all his own—young and fresh and full of rebellion. Yet the whole was bigger than the sum of its parts, and there was something about him that you couldn't explain—a level of magnetism that was rare. Brando had it in his early career, and maybe the Beatles, but even the great

Bruce Springsteen did not. Petty was rolling now. His eyes were alive with imagination and fun, and the two women with him were hanging on his words.

Later, they wondered what they expected. Maybe they had stereotyped race drivers, sold them short as human beings who thought about nothing but speed and cars and answered every question with a grunt. Whatever they expected, it was not Kyle Petty, who wrote stories for his children and songs for his wife; who collected first-edition books and whose knowledge was scattered in so many directions. They heard, of course, that that was his problem. He liked to dabble in too many things, and didn't have the focus to be a great driver. That was the rap around the NASCAR garage, but by the time they came to the race in Dover, Hudson and Jetton were certain it was wrong. They had heard Petty talk about it too many times—how his injury had made his ambition more intense—and as they watched him regain his physical strength, they could see in his driving that it was more than just talk.

As they stared out at the rain still falling in Dover, they knew the next few races were important. It had been disappointing not to win in Charlotte, but the fact that they came so close was encouraging. They had jumped from 21st to 13th in points. It was crucial now to keep moving up.

The rain finally stopped on Sunday afternoon. The skies overhead were gray and soggy, but NASCAR's radar reports were encouraging. There was a hole in the front and a chance to race, and at 12:50 P.M., they were able to start. Petty was squarely in the middle of the pack, starting 16th and moving up slowly. He passed Bill Elliott and Harry Gant, and set his sights on Rusty Wallace. Unfortunately, after twenty-seven laps, the rains returned and the cars continued around the track under caution. About that time, they discovered a problem. Robin could see that a piece of paper, maybe some kind of concession stand wrapping, was sticking to the grill of Petty's Pontiac. Two laps later, the paper was still there. They remembered the disaster from the race in Darlington when the car overheated from tape and rubber on the grill. "I don't want this thing to burn up," said Petty, and they decided to pit to get rid of the paper. While they were at it, they changed four tires and filled the car up with gas, and returned to the track in 32nd place.

Still the rains continued, and the caution dragged on for nineteen laps. By then, nearly everyone needed to pit, and when all but a handful of cars came in, Petty stayed out and was in 6th place. It was a piece of pure luck, jumping twenty-six spots without doing a thing, but Robin came on the radio and laughed. "I love it when a plan comes together," he said.

In the pit, they hoped it was an omen for the day, and for seventy-five laps that's how it appeared. When the race restarted, Petty moved quickly into 5th place, and within four laps he passed Dale Jarrett and moved up to 4th. He was flying now, passing Greg Sacks for 3rd and chasing Kulwicki and the leader, Ricky Rudd. He made it to 2nd before his tires got slick and his car began to fade, but he was still in good shape on lap 120 as he came up behind the slow car of Dave Marcis. Marcis was one of the veterans on the circuit, an eccentric, gray-haired man of fifty-one, who was starting his 696th race. He had won only five, but he was there every week, battling away in underfunded cars that almost never had a chance at Victory Lane. His proudest moment came in 1982 when he won in Richmond in a car that should never have come even close. Kyle Petty liked him because he was different. He raced every week in wing-tip shoes (he said it kept his feet from getting too hot), and you could count on him being a little cantankerous, racing hard, squeezing everything he could from his car.

On the 120th lap in Dover, Marcis was getting ready to pit. He raised his hand to signal his intentions, but he saw a puddle at the edge of the pit road, and had to pull out again to get around it. Petty was passing at precisely that moment, and he pulled down low to the best groove on the track, expecting Marcis to be out of the way. Their cars ran together, and Petty went spinning into the wall.

The damage was awful, and Felix Sabates could hardly believe it. The whole month of May had been going so well, and in Dover they were headed for a top 5 finish. But now it was ruined by a driver like Marcis, who was always out there getting in the way. "I just don't understand the stupid idiot," Sabates told a crew from TNN. "That's not racing. The guy is an idiot, has always been an idiot, and will continue to be an idiot. As long as NASCAR lets people like him get on the track, you are going to have this kind of problem. He shouldn't be racing."

The Cuban Tornado was loose once again, like Ricky Ricardo in a mad Latin rage, and people all over the country were shocked. It was one thing when he blew up at Bobby Hillin in the pits, or even when he decided to chew out his own team. Those moments were private, and easily sanitized by the press. This, however, was a tantrum on national TV, a violation of the gentlemanly code of racing, and it was all the more glaring when the cameras switched to Kyle. Petty was trying to save his car, which had been dragged by the wrecker to the far end of the garage, with pieces of metal falling off along the way. He and Robin were both looking frantic. The damage was bad enough as it was—broken oil pump, fuel pump and radiator, and the left side suspension completely in shreds. The walls in Dover were the hardest in the sport. As Buddy Baker once said, "When you hit these things, everything stops but the fillings in your teeth." Kyle and Robin, however, were determined to get the car back on the track, and the guy in the wrecker didn't seem to understand. He was dragging the ruins to the wrong end of the garage with Petty running after him pounding on his hood. It was about that time that the cameras arrived— Glenn Jarrett and his crew from TNN, asking Kyle to talk about the wreck.

Petty took a breath and forced a smile and said the accident was nobody's fault: "Dave waved his hand to pit so I went to the outside of him, and evidently while he was waving his hand he hit something and just skated up the race track a little bit. There was nothing he could do . . . It was just one of those things."

Jarrett told Kyle he was being "mighty gracious," but it was a ritual, of course, that everyone expected. Racing was a sport where people made mistakes; Petty himself had made his share, and you didn't unload on a veteran like Marcis. The first casualty of whining was a driver's own image, and Petty had learned from his father's example that an image was something to take care of. Beyond that, it was simply a matter of class—making yourself say the right thing under pressure, knowing that eventually you'd come to believe it.

It was a lesson that Felix would learn in a hurry, and he would later apologize to Dave Marcis. His style was to get mad and then move on, never holding a grudge because of anger he suppressed. In the meantime, Sabates became a pariah for the next several weeks, showered by criticism from the fans, who questioned whether he, not Marcis, belonged in the sport.

The team, meanwhile, patched the car back together. It was not an easy job. The frame was mangled in so many places that they had to blow-torch it to put a fuel pump on. They pulled the bent sheet metal out of the way, and put in the pumps and then rebuilt the left suspension system. The whole job took them more than two hours, but amazingly enough at 4:22 they were able to crank it. Kyle climbed in and returned to the track while the people in the grandstands cheered in disbelief. He was 215 laps behind the leaders and five seconds slower every time around the track. His car looked ridiculous without a hood and a few other pieces—and there was a place where the floor was torn away, and his tires were slinging globs of rubber through the hole. It stung when it hit him on the shoulder and arm, leaving red whelps on his tricep muscle. But Petty didn't mind. He stood to gain five positions in the race, moving from 34th to 29th place by completing more laps than the other wrecked cars. He would gain fifteen points in the standings for the season, and he knew it might be important later on. He felt good about that, but more than anything else, he was proud of the team. It would have been easy for the guys to give it up—to examine the wreckage and call it a day, but instead everyone of them behaved like pros.

"You guys did it," he told them at the end. "You're the ones that picked up the points."

Back in the pits Robin Pemberton smiled. It was a funny thing about racing—you could finish third in Charlotte and feel disappointed, 29th in Dover and feel pretty good. It didn't take long for perspective to return. Their stop in Charlotte had been a major step forward, and however you cut it Dover was not. They lost ground at a track where they expected to gain, and they were not optimistic about the race coming up. The next one was Sonoma—a road course on the fringes of California's Napa Valley, with hills and turns in both directions, different from anything they had run so far. Kyle hadn't raced there in nearly two years—his broken leg kept him out in 1991—and when they went out to practice a couple of weeks earlier, the results were not encouraging. Petty wrecked the car his first time around—tore it up so badly there was nothing to do but turn around and come home. They could only hope for better when it came time to race.

Despite the difficulties that loomed just ahead, Richard Bostic looked forward to the trip across country. Bostic, truck driver for the Kyle Petty team, loved his gleaming, million-dollar payload— the hand-polished truck with the Mello Yello logo and the racing stripes of red, yellow and green. They cut quite a figure on the interstate roads, and Bostic had friends all over the country whom he had met with the help of his CB radio. "How about you, Mello Yello?" the other truckers would say, and their conversations crackled through the nightime hours.

Bostic is one of the friendliest people on the circuit, a handsome man, still trim and muscled at the age of forty-five, with curly brown hair and a sandy mustache that resembled Kyle Petty's. He had been around racing for most of his life. For years he was a fixture on the short track circuit, and one grand night in the 1980s he won a Late Model race at the Fayetteville Speedway, leading the event from first lap to last. He wondered sometimes if he could have made it to the top, maybe with a break or two here and there. But trucking was also in his blood; his daddy had done it, and from the day he was old enough to drive, Bostic fell in love with the days and nights on the road, meeting new people while the country unfolded before his eyes.

The run to Sonoma was one of his favorites. They would form an armada—Bostic and the truckers from the other race teams— meeting most often at the Unocal station just off the interstate in Amarillo, Texas. As they headed west along I-40, there was always something unexpected to see—the silhouette of a tree on the Panhandle horizon, the snow on the mountains in the middle of Arizona. Sometimes they would cross the Mojave at night and hit the Napa Valley just after sunrise. The track was on the western fringe of the valley, where the wineries gave way to steep hillsides, and the grass turned golden with the first hint of summer. There was not a prettier place on the circuit.

The track, however, was tricky to drive, with thirteen turns and cars running clockwise for the first time all year. Petty had never won a road course race. There are only two on the Winston Cup circuit (the other is at Watkins Glen, New York), and only a handful of drivers—Ricky Rudd, Rusty Wallace, and Ernie Irvan—seemed to have them mastered. But Bostic thought Kyle could join those ranks. He was smooth enough, which was what it took, and his rhythm was obviously returning as he practiced. He qualified 19th, which was not that good, but when other cars were out there with him, he was as fast as anybody. "The car is really good," Petty told one reporter. "Ricky could get in it, or Rusty, and go really fast. Me? . . . " He shrugged and said they'd just have to see.

As they waited for the race to start Sunday morning, a momentous piece of news hit the NASCAR garage. Bill France, Sr., was dead in Florida. In a way, it didn't come as much of a shock. The old man was eighty-two. Still, until it happened, a lot of people would have told you that the founder of NASCAR was too tough to die.

France was not a beloved figure, despite what his eulogists were already saying, but it was hard to find people who didn't respect him. He was a tall, craggy-faced man who burst on the scene as a driver and promoter when racing was still a disorganized sport. In 1947, he called a meeting of track owners and promoters to talk about bringing some order to the chaos. The result of that gathering in Daytona Beach was a new sanctioning body they called NASCAR—the National Association of Stock Car Auto Racing. Some people at the meeting thought the name was stupid, redundant in its use of "auto" and "car," but France liked the acronym and prevailed.

That's the way it's been in racing ever since, as France gradually took control of NASCAR, buying up the shares of the other founding partners. He built new tracks, and pushed for bigger purses for the drivers, and guided the sport from its raw early days as a Southern pastime. Nobody denies that France was successful. All you have to do is look at the numbers—the sold-out tracks from coast to coast and the national television audience every week. However, France was not a benevolent czar—especially not with those who crossed him.

Richard Petty found out the hard way. In 1969, he tried to organize a drivers' union. It was not the first time the attempt had been made. In the early sixties, superstar drivers Tim Flock and Curtis Turner called on Jimmy Hoffa and the Teamsters to help put together a drivers' association that would demand more money. Hoffa was ecstatic, promising great things, but France called all the drivers together and threatened to close every track on the circuit. According to one account, he was packing a pistol as he told the drivers they were going to starve and banned both Flock and Turner from the sport. The drivers backed down, but their grievances remained, and a few years later they tried again. Their primary issue this time was safety—particularly at the new Talladega Speedway, where speeds were approaching 200 m.p.h. and tires were coming apart at the seams. The drivers' union, with Richard Petty as president, asked France to postpone the Talladega race until the engineers at Goodyear could invent a safer tire. When France refused, most top drivers, including Petty, packed up their cars and headed for home. France was undaunted. He called in the scabs and the race went ahead precisely on schedule, with an unknown driver named Richard Brickhouse winning the only race of his major-league career. France retired in 1985, turning NASCAR over to his son, Bill Jr., who rules with a somewhat subtler hand. But the legacy and memory of his toughness survive, and the NASCAR garage was somber when he died.

"He was hardheaded enough to keep the sport going in the way he wanted," Kyle Petty concluded, speaking softly to a cluster of reporters. "You had to respect him."

A few hours later, the race began—precisely on time. Before it started, Robin confided that his personal expectations were modest—"Just a decent finish," he said, "We'll gain some experience and be better next time."—but the first few laps made him hope for more. Kyle passed three cars the first time around the track, and still another on lap number 2. "Good work!" exclaimed Steve Knipe, the spotter. "Get 'em one at a time." Petty did, moving all the way to 6th by the 31st lap, with Dale Earnhardt the next car ahead. The fans, of course, were on their feet. They always are when there's a battle on the track involving Earnhardt. With his intimidator image, he's a villain to some and a hero to others who admire his nerve, but almost nobody finds him boring. This time he was trying to hold his position as Petty pulled beside him going into turn 7. They were two abreast going up the hill with Petty on the outside as they hit the S-turns. Petty made it past as they started down the hill, but he could see as he glanced in his rearview mirror that Ernie Irvan was gaining on them both. Ernie was amazing. He had jumped the gun at the start of the race, and by way of a penalty NASCAR had put him at the end of the field. Now here he was in thirty-three laps, battling for 6th position in the race. He got around Earnhardt and set his sights on Kyle, and Petty could see that he was gaining in a hurry. Within a lap, Ernie was past him and continuing to battle his way to the front. There was not another car on the track that could touch him, but Petty couldn't worry about that now. He was still trying to fashion a decent finish of his own, even though his car was beginning to change. Little by little, after he pushed it to the limit in passing Earnhardt, he could feel it becoming less responsive in the turns. He could see that Earnhardt was gaining again, and so were a couple of other cars just behind him.

Earnhardt passed him on lap 40, and Kyle faded slowly from seventh to tenth before his real problems started with ten laps to go. With the car handling poorly, he locked the brakes going into a turn and flat-spotted a tire—burned away enough rubber in one particular spot that the wheel began to vibrate badly. At one point near the end of the race, the vibration was so severe that Petty lost control and skidded off the track. He managed to get the car going again, and held on desperately for the last several laps. He finished 12th, half a lap behind the winner, Ernie Irvan, and apologized to Robin and the crew. "Sorry about that, man," he said.

Robin told him not to worry. "We'll get better with time," he insisted. But he also knew, without having to say it, that if they were going to salvage anything from the season, they needed to make some progress soon.

In Pocono, they did. Petty ran a smooth and efficient race on this track in the mountains of eastern Pennsylvania. In other seasons it's snow-ski country, but in the middle of June the back roads leading to the Pocono Speedway are choked with caravans of race fans. The track itself is deep in the hills—a large, flat oval of two and a half miles with banking in the turns of 6 degrees. Once again, Petty hadn't been there in nearly two years, and he told a reporter before the race that he didn't expect to do very well. "We've got a good team," he said. "I'm just behind. One of these days, we'll be all right."

That day came quickly as Petty started 5th and finished 6th. In between he was almost always in the top 10. He faded to 11th early in the race when the car was too tight and pushing in the turns, but they made some adjustments and he was quickly back to 6th, where he stayed for most of the rest of the day. He made it as high as 2nd one time, and later he faded as far back as 9th. Then with good pit stops he climbed back to 6th, and coasted home for his easiest finish of the year.

The Pocono race, with its satisfying ending, was squarely in the heart of a difficult stretch. On consecutive weekends, the NASCAR tour had crisscrossed the country—from Delaware to California, then back to Pennsylvania—and it was not over yet. The following weekend they headed for the Michigan International Speedway in the lush green hills just west of Detroit. Robin was optimistic. They were using the same car that had done well in Charlotte—the sleek Pontiac they had built in the spring. Robin was eager to run it again, but he knew that Michigan was a very different track. It was a two-mile oval, bigger than Charlotte, but not quite as fast because the banking on the turns was not as steep. It required a different setup of springs and shocks, and on the first day of practice they struggled to find it. Somehow, they missed. Petty was mediocre on his qualifying lap, and on Sunday he started the race 17th.

Nobody was quite sure what to expect. They had made some improvements in the late practice rounds, but Kyle again was adjusting to a track he hadn't run in two years. All they knew was that they needed a good finish. After Martinsville, when they had fallen to 21st in the season's point standings, Robin told the guys on the team not to worry. The key, he said, was to make the top ten by Watkins Glen, a road course race the second week in August. "If we can do that," he insisted, "we can make the top 5 by the end of the year." They had been chipping away at it since Talladega, two steps forward for every step back, and they had moved to 15th place after Pocono. Now it was critically important to preserve their momentum—to avoid the bad luck that had hit them in Dover, or the fade at the end that had hurt them in Sonoma.

Robin was antsy on the morning of the race. The Michigan weather was erratic, unseasonably cold, with clouds settling in then drifting away, which made it even trickier to set up the car. Fortunately, things started well. Within a few laps, Petty was charging once again through the field. By the halfway point he was in 6th place, and ten laps later he made the top 5. It looked almost like a repeat of Pocono—Petty moving easily through the string of cars, passing high or low, it didn't seem to matter. Then with fifty laps to go, things began to get tense. There was a caution on the track, and the leaders came in for gas and new tires. One of the fastest cars was Darrell Waltrip's, which raised an interesting question of strategy. Already in the race, Waltrip had gone forty-six laps on a tank of gas, farther than most of the other contenders. When the race restarted with forty-nine to go, everybody faced a difficult dilemma. If Waltrip tried to make it without another stop, should the other teams try to do the same? Or should they take the time for a final pit stop, hoping that Waltrip would run out of gas?

In the Kyle Petty pit, Robin was hoping to avoid that decision. Petty was never very good at conserving his fuel—not as smooth with the accelerator as Waltrip. He was inclined to stomp it, squirting extra fuel in the carburator jets, which meant that he ran through his gas in a hurry and probably couldn't make it to the end of the race. But if, somehow, they could catch another caution, then everyone could pit and the problem with gasoline would disappear.

Those were Robin's thoughts as the race restarted—and sure enough, a caution flag appeared. Coming out of a turn after less than two laps, Harry Gant went high on the track, and his car began to slide in loose asphalt. It was the same thing Kyle had done in Bristol, getting caught in the loose stuff next to the wall, and Gant began to spin in a cloud of smoke. Amazingly enough, he didn't hit anything, but the caution flag was out and the leaders rushed to the pits for more gas.

The problem was, it was still too early. They would have to cover forty-five laps when the race went green, which was ninety miles, and Robin was afraid that was still too much. Race cars get about four miles a gallon, give or take, depending on conditions. With twenty-two gallons of gas in the tank, that meant eighty-eight miles between fillups. They had a computer in the pit to do the math more precisely, and Bob Romano was feeding in the numbers. Romano was a first-year member of the Kyle Petty crew, and he didn't want to blow it. He's a quiet man, a pilot by training, whose primary job was to fly the team to races. He also worked every week calculating the gas, entering the data on quantity and mileage and letting the computer spit out its conclusions. The news this time was not very good. Based on the mileage they were getting so far, they would run out of gas on the next to last lap. The computer was emphatic on that point, but Bob Romano was not so sure. They had made allowances in the computer program for gas that sloshed from the car as it was filled: A full tank of gas was 21.5 instead of twenty-two gallons, which the tank really held. It was a safe way to figure, but Romano noticed on the last pit stop that the crew barely spilled any gas at all. He told Robin Pemberton, perhaps with a little more conviction than he felt: "We can make it."

Robin was still not certain he believed it. Out on the track, Kyle was pushing as hard as he could, using up the gas supply in a hurry. There was no way around it. Davey Allison was leading the race—his car was easily the strongest out there—but Kyle had a chance for a top 5 finish. He was racing Ricky Rudd and Ted Musgrave, and both of them were fast. With ten laps to go, the tension was heavy and it got even worse when Musgrave decided to pit for gas. That assured Kyle of a top 5 finish—unless, of course, the computer was right.

The computer was wrong. They finished the race on the last fumes of gas, and Kyle passed Rudd on the final lap. He came in fourth. Romano smiled, and the rest of the guys on the crew were ecstatic. It was their second strong race in as many weekends, which gave them a feeling of genuine momentum and moved them all the way to 11th in the points. They knew they were not the best team on the circuit—not yet, anyway. Davey Allison was headed toward his finest year ever. He had won four races and was leading comfortably in the points competition. Bill Elliott, too, was doing very well. He was second in the points and had four wins—and Ernie Irvan was getting stronger all the time.

By contrast, the Petty crew had struggled, with wrecks and other problems early in the season. But they had five top tens in the past seven races, and Robin could see they were starting to believe.

It was a nice way to end the first half of the year.

CHAPTER 8

MEMORIES OF THE KING

There was a piece of history before the second half began. The NASCAR boys made a side trip to Indy—not everybody, just nine drivers specially selected to test stock cars at the most historic track in the country. The Indianapolis Motor Speedway opened its gates in 1911, and it had an aura like nothing else in the sport. The Indy cars were earthbound rockets, with open cockpits and uncovered wheels—lightweight contraptions that easily broke two-hundred miles per hour. Earlier in 1992, Roberto Guerrero set a new track record of 232.482, winning the pole for the 76th running of the Indianapolis 500. A few days later, he became a permanent part of Indy lore by wrecking his car before the race even started. He hit the wall on the first parade lap, swerving back and forth to put heat in his tires. Even that was a colorful piece of history, and the NASCAR drivers were obviously in awe when they arrived at the track on June 22.

Nobody had ever raced a stock car at Indy, and a lot of people assumed they never would. There had been some speculation a few months earlier when NASCAR president Bill France, Jr., and his Indianapolis counterpart, Tony George, appeared together at a gathering of racing writers in Charlotte. They were asked about the possibility of NASCAR at Indy, and France responded with a litany of problems—the added cost, the difficulty of finding an open date, etc. George, however, was more tantalizing. "I really enjoy NASCAR racing," he said. And now here they were, nine drivers ready to take the track—a magnificent oval, two and a half miles with broad straightaways and sharp, flat turns at either end. The test was clearly a step toward a race, and Kyle wasn't sure how he felt about it. Would they be tampering somehow with a sacred tradition? Would you race quarter horses at Churchill Downs?

Whatever the answer, it was somebody else's decision to make, and if the stock cars were coming to Indianapolis, Petty was delighted to be a pioneer. On the opening day of testing he took his video camera with him, and spent a few hours putting things on tape. He got the other drivers as they arrived at the track, and crew members working underneath their cars, and then a few stills of the speedway itself: the vast straightaway, and Al Unser's pit, and the row of bricks at the start-finish line—historic remnants of the track's early days. He was rolling now, and he headed to the stands where more than ten thousand people were waiting. "How about a wave?" he yelled, and the people obliged. They had never seen a driver like this. The Indy guys were splendid, but aloof, and here was Petty with his video cam, wanting to take his own pictures of the fans. When the practice ended a few hours later, they surged to the fence to shake his hand, and he stood for two hours signing autographs.

Petty wasn't alone in reaching out. Ricky Rudd, Mark Martin, really all of the others did the same. But as Robin Pemberton watched from the crowd, he couldn't help thinking that Kyle was different. He was so at ease in these public settings—so completely himself, no matter what craziness was swirling around him. Robin kept thinking of the word "charisma," but it was not quite right. It was trite and insubstantial somehow, particularly when he thought of other moments from the year. Back in Martinsville, for example, Kyle had spent time with Travis McCauley, who was nine years old and blind, and who had written him a personal letter in braille. A few months earlier, a friend had told Kyle that Travis was a fan, and asked him to make a tape for Christmas. Kyle agreed and spent a little time fiddling around with a cassette, talking to Travis and singing him songs. Travis played the tape until he wore it out, then came to the track to meet Petty in person. They talked for a while, and a few minutes later Petty led Travis over to the car where he could trace the contours of it with his fingers.

"It doesn't feel like a forty-two," the boy said finally, when he came to the number that was stenciled on the door.

"No," said Petty, "but let me show you."

He took the small fingers gently in his own, and guided them once again around the number. "Right there," he said. "That's why it's confusing. The four and the two are all joined together."

Robin was struck by the scene, and he knew it was not an isolated event. Back in February, Kyle and Ernie Irvan drove from Daytona to St. Petersburg, Florida, to visit Tyler Sontag, a seven-year-old on a life-support system. A few months later, Tyler was better, and able to visit the track in his mechanized wheelchair. Petty saw him first. "Hey, Ernie," he yelled. "Look who came to see us this time." Irvan trotted over and squatted by the wheelchair, and he and Petty thanked Tyler for coming.

Robin was glad that moments like that were a part of racing. Maybe they were a part of other sports too. If so, that was good. Fame could magnify simple acts of kindness—a fact that the Pettys had grasped early on. Richard, in fact, had set the standard for everybody else with his warm and ongoing interaction with the fans. But Robin thought Kyle might one day surpass him. For one thing, Kyle wore his compassion much closer to the surface, and in less emotional settings like the one in Indianapolis, where the fans simply wanted to reach out and touch him, he had a fun-loving presence that was hard to resist—a style at least as magnetic as his father's.

That, at least, was Robin's point of view, and as the year wore on, a curious thought began to form in his mind: If they could reach the point where they were winning more consistently, three or four races a year and maybe a championship now and then, there would be no limit to Kyle Petty's fame.

"This kid," thought Robin, "could really be big." Maybe, one day, even bigger than his daddy.

Two weeks later, the thought was heresy as the tour moved south to Daytona Beach. Nobody was bigger in Daytona than Richard Petty. He was clearly into his homestretch as a driver, as NASCAR began the second half of the season. Generally speaking, the circuit stopped twice at each track, which meant that the Pepsi 400 on July 4 would be the King's last run at the Daytona Speedway. The nostalgia was heavy—and all the more so because July 2 was Petty's birthday. He was fifty-five, too old to be driving a stock car for a living, but still the fans were hoping for something grand. Daytona, after all, was the place where Petty got his 200th win. It had been a glorious occasion, July 4, 1984, with President Reagan watching from the stands. Even then, Petty was forty-seven and well past his prime, so maybe they could hope for one more miracle—one more improbable display of greatness by the man who had given them so many thrills.

On qualifying day, they almost got it. The King was the seventh driver to take the track, and his speed was startling—the fastest of the day at 188.961. Petty had won 123 poles in his career, more than anybody in the sport, but he hadn't accomplished the feat in awhile—not since July of '79. It was hard to imagine he might do it again, but one by one the other drivers fell short—Ricky Rudd, Davey Allison, Kyle, Harry Gant. Some of them were more than a half second slower.

"How about the King?" exclaimed Michael Waltrip as he completed an impressive run of his own. Michael, the affable younger brother of Darrell Waltrip, had special reasons to be happy for Richard Petty. Back in 1984, when he was a struggling driver trying to find a ride, Michael moved to North Carolina. The Pettys took him in; he lived first with Kyle, and then for nine months with Richard and Lynda. He didn't know what to expect from the King—knew him only as his brother's archrival, a fierce and overbearing competitor whom Darrell had complained about for years—but the

Petty household was a warm surprise. Richard's wife, Lynda, was one of the kindest people he had met, and the King himself was remarkably laid-back. Most times in the evenings after one of Lynda's dinners, they would pile on the couch with a bowl of popcorn and the TV rumbling until it was time to go to bed. Michael felt sort of like the King's other son, and the amazing thing was Richard and Lynda were so relaxed about it—so completely unimpressed with the gesture they were making. As Richard would put it a few years later, "The boy just needed a place to stay."

Michael remembered all that at the Daytona Speedway when it looked like Richard was going to win the pole, but just as he exclaimed, "How about the King?", driver Sterling Marlin took the track. Marlin was fast; everybody knew that. He had won the Daytona pole in February, and his car in practice had been one of the best. His first lap was 47.78 seconds, about a tenth slower than Petty's best lap, but his second time around he picked up the pace. He beat Petty's time by a tenth of a second. Poor Sterling Marlin. He emerged from his car to a shower of boos, and told the bewildered members of his crew: "Boys, I think I done messed up." The fans in the stands could hardly believe it. How could a nobody like Sterling Marlin, a man who had never even won a race, rob them of a moment so perfect and grand? They could see it already: Richard Petty on the pole for one last time, maybe leading early and even winning the race. Stranger things had happened, but here was Marlin out doing his job and messing up a piece of history in the making. Even a few drivers had trouble comprehending. Did Sterling not have any imagination, no poetry in his soul?

"I think I might have lifted," said Darrell Waltrip. "This is like the guy that shot Santa Claus."

Starting second, however, was still no small accomplishment. In racing, they called it the outside pole, and Richard Petty had now won 140. He was still the talk of the town in Daytona.

More than ten thousand people gathered that night to celebrate his birthday—and two days later the President of the United States came to town. It was an awesome moment in the NASCAR garage, as Air Force One soared quietly overhead, the great white plane against a blue sky, and the emblem of the country stenciled on the side. A few minutes later, President Bush disembarked from his black limousine, looking tanned and relaxed, smiling happily at the waves of applause. "This president," he said, "comes to greet a King."

A few feet away, Kyle Petty watched the scene with his daughter, Montgomery Lee, on his shoulders. This was not the first president to pay homage to his father. Years ago, when Kyle was still in elementary school, Richard Petty was invited to the White House. Richard Nixon was president at the time, and he said nice things, and when the account of the visit hit the local newspapers, everybody at school was amazed. Kyle hadn't said a word about it—not to his teacher, not to his principal, not to the other kids in his class. His parents had told him never to brag. They had taught him over and over again that Richard Petty had a different kind of job—but it was *different*, not better, than the jobs of other fathers who were plumbers or farmers or clerks at the store. Later, when Kyle himself was a man, he would come to understand, would come to know how remarkable that was, and his eyes sometimes would glisten with pride. Even then, he would try to be modest, deflecting the compliments about his father's humility. "This sport will keep you humble," he would say—but he had seen enough of the arrogance of athletes to know that his father's attitude was different. However you cut it, it was simply a fact: Very few people attained the fame of Richard Petty without somehow being altered at the core.

The King, however, was always the same. He was as gracious with the fans as he was with the President of the United States. Everybody who knew him agreed on that. But if his story to that point was simple and good, beneath the surface it was more complicated. For one thing, he was always something of an absentee father—a man caught up in the demands of his career, in that hell-for-leather world of big-time racing where they crisscrossed the country and sometimes partied as hard as they raced. The temptations were everywhere—particularly the women, with their supple bodies and willing dispositions—and more than a few racing families fell apart. Richard Petty's did not. His deepest passions were reserved for the track, where he was fiercely competitive, and where in his prime in the 1970s, he was not always beloved by his peers.

His battles with Bobby Allison were legendary, and when Darrell Waltrip burst upon the scene, brash and talented, a young pretender to the stock car throne, he didn't feel much welcome from the King.

"I guess," said Waltrip, "my earliest memory of Richard was his long, bent forefinger right in my chest—and him saying, 'Boy . . . ,' always telling me what I was doing wrong. It's a fond memory now, but I see that big ole finger in my dreams."

Meanwhile, for Petty's children, it was a strange way to grow up. Kyle was the oldest, and he had three sisters—Sharon, Lisa and Rebecca, all of whom worried about their father. In the course of his thirty-five years on the track, Richard was involved in some soul-chilling crashes, his car flipping wildly and flying apart. Almost literally, at one time or another, he broke every bone from his neck to his toes (his neck twice), and as his children grew older, the dangers of the sport became more real. Aside from that, there were ordinary things—school functions that their father was unable to attend, and long summers that the family would spend on the road. There was always a certain monotony about it, as the motel rooms began to run together and Sundays at the track were a noisy routine. Still, as a family the Pettys were close, and as the children look back, they give a large measure of the credit to their mother. Lynda Petty was the glue. She took them to parks and museums on the road, and almost never missed a function at school—and when they needed somebody to listen she was there.

In Lynda's mind, that was particularly important for Kyle, who seemed so confident and carefree on the surface, even as a boy. His mother understood that the confidence was real—the natural outgrowth of intelligence and popularity—but she also believed that it served as a mask. "Inside," she says, "Kyle is a sensitive and sometimes insecure young man. Underneath his shell is a boy that needs to be told that he's done good. And in this family, I was the one who passed out the praise."

She pauses now, for this is tricky ground, but then she plunges ahead with the story. "Richard," she says, "is a wonderful man. But he holds back. I don't guess his mama and daddy ever told him that he had done good either. If they ever did, I never saw it.

For some people, it's hard to put their arm around you and say, 'I love you.' My family was always the hugging kind. Richard's family was not like that."

The greatest irony in Lynda Petty's mind was that Richard could muster such warmth for the fans. Every day, the mail brought reminders—people who were touched by his kindness through the years and just had to write to say they remembered. Perhaps the most famous reminiscence of all came from the basketball player, Brad Daugherty, an all-pro center for the Cleveland Cavaliers. He grew up in the mountains of North Carolina—stock car country—and even though he was black and most people connected with the sport were white, he was always a fan. Once in the early 1970s, his father took him to a race in Daytona, and they were standing outside the chain-link fence that separates the garage from the infield crowd. All of a sudden, they saw Richard Petty, who had emerged from behind his #43 car and was walking briskly in the opposite direction. Brad, who was still in elementary school, began to call out: "Hey, Mr. Petty. Hey, Mr. Petty!"

Petty turned and saw the little boy, then flashed a smile and walked to the fence. He squatted and talked for nearly ten minutes, as if he had nothing else to do. It was vintage Richard Petty, reaching out, refusing to set himself apart, taking gentle care of the feelings of a child. Lynda Petty was proud of her husband for that, but she knew that such interactions were painless. They required some patience, and a concern about people that came from his heart, but no real emotion to be worn on his sleeve. Reaching out to a son, however, telling him face to face that you loved him—that, somehow, was a whole different story.

Richard himself was asked about it once. He was sitting in the bus that he takes to the track, a homey place with wood-paneled walls and soft leather furniture, and bagels and Oreo cookies on the counter. Petty was lounging in his favorite chair, while a stream of interviewers moved in and out. Some of them were nervous, apologizing for intruding on his time, but the King merely smiled, taking the questions and the people as they came. He said he was proud of the son they had raised—proud of his intelligence and ability in a car, proud of his gift for dealing with people.

"Oh man, yeah, I'm proud," he said, and then he admitted in a wistful aside: "But I don't tell him. I'm not an emotional person. I don't show my emotions on the outside. That's a real big fault of mine. When Kyle wins a race, I just beam. But I don't tell him. His mother, though, she pats him all the time."

Some people say there's a barrier there, created inevitably by Richard's reserve, and that Kyle is still much closer to his mother. Certainly, it's true that he communicates with her, tells her things he wouldn't confide elsewhere. But Kyle and his father are also close—closer perhaps than they have ever been. It was funny how things had finally come together. They were starting the second half of Richard's final year, while the season for Kyle was more like a beginning. His career could have ended with the wreck in Talladega, but it didn't, and now he was back more focused than ever: more like his father. His team had jelled over the past several races, and he had a good feeling about what lay ahead—about the possibility of adding to the legacy of his name. Whatever the frailties that went along with it, it was a gift, he knew, too precious to squander.

When race day came it was miserably hot, the way the summers usually are in Daytona—the temperature approaching 100 degrees and the humidity so high the air felt like soup. All week long, the guys on the team had been a little snappish, especially Robin, who was furious at his truck driver, Richard Bostic. Before they left Charlotte, Robin made a list of gears for Bostic to bring, and he wrote it down on a sheet of paper—*290–307*, which meant that he wanted those gears and everything in between. Bostic, however, had misunderstood, and brought only the 290 and the 307. "You're a grown man," Robin snapped, and Bostic, one of the gentler souls in racing, blushed deep red from embarrassment and hurt. He didn't argue, though. He respected Robin for telling him straight, and he also understood his frustration. The car wasn't running well on the track. They had had a problem with it in inspection: NASCAR ruled that their bumper was wide, and when they shaved it down, it seemed to play hell with the aerodynamics. Robin was trying everything to compensate, including several changes in the gear ratios. They had made some progress, but on the morning of the race he was still not happy. He knew there were other cars that were faster.

When the race began, one of those cars belonged to Richard Petty. He surged to the lead from the outside pole, and after two laps he was pulling away. It was like old times—the King in his Pontiac setting the pace, the first time he had managed to do it all year. The crowd was hooked, a hundred thousand people on their feet screaming, pleading, hoping against hope for a finish to remember—but the storybook ending wilted in the sun. Petty lost the lead after only five laps, and at the halfway point he quit the race, his aging body overcome by the heat.

Kyle, meanwhile, was hanging in there. He started 12th and moved up to 7th in the first ten laps, but Dale Jarrett passed him on lap 11, and by lap 13 he had faded to 10th. He was beginning to lose the lead draft of cars, nine of them punching a hole in the air, and he continued to fade for the next thirty laps. His car was tight and unresponsive in the turns, and after his first pit stop on lap 45, he had dropped back all the way to 23rd. They put in a spring rubber to loosen the chassis, and suddenly he was fast and passing other cars—Rick Mast, Jimmy Hensley, Terry Labonte. By lap 95, he was back to 15th, but then disaster struck in the pits. The engine choked, and he couldn't get it started, and by the time it finally cranked he was more than a lap behind the leader, Ernie Irvan.

A few laps later, he almost wrecked. Morgan Shepherd lost control and set off a chain reaction of crashes, with Petty in the middle of a mass of spinning cars. He hit the brakes and dove down low all the way to the grass, and somehow made it through without a scratch.

"Good job, Kyle," said Steve Knipe, the spotter.

"Damn, it was close," said Petty in reply.

Now there were thirty-five laps to go, and Petty was 14th when they restarted the race. That was where he finished. He made it as high as 13th place, but Darrell Waltrip passed him with eight laps to go. Ernie Irvan won the race, and Sterling Marlin finished 2nd, which was becoming a habit. He had done it seven times in the course of his career, without ever making it to Victory Lane. For Kyle, of course, it was a mediocre day, and the guys on the crew were glad it was over. They had a week off before heading back to Pocono, where at least they knew it wouldn't be as hot.

CHAPTER 9

THE ROAD TO VICTORY LANE

He went to bed late on July 17, the night before his qualifying run at Pocono. The mountains, once again, were full of race fans, clamoring for autographs and pictures. Thankfully, his suite was quiet at the Camelback Chateau. His youngest son Austin was asleep in the loft, exhausted after all the excitement of the day. It was a special weekend for him—a trip all alone to the races with his dad. His brother, Adam, was going to Talladega, and their little sister, Montgomery Lee, would get her turn on the next trip to Michigan. It was a tradition they had started in the Petty family, a way to spend more time with the kids. But now it was late, and the TV was flickering on CNN—recaps of the Democratic National Convention. Kyle was intrigued by the images of Bill Clinton, this handsome and energetic governor of Arkansas who wanted to be president of the United States.

Petty, ordinarily, was not political—not like his father, who was a staunch and passionate Ronald Reagan conservative, a friend of presidents from Nixon to Bush, with the exception of Jimmy Carter in between. Richard Petty even served as a county commissioner, and some people said, when his racing career was over, that he had a political future if he wanted it. Kyle didn't have much interest in that. He hadn't even voted in the last few elections. But when politics touched on larger themes—the environment, poverty, maybe the fight against AIDS—all of a sudden he began to pay attention. He liked Bill Clinton—liked his talk about ending division and trying to do something for people in need. "When it comes to social issues," Petty told one reporter, "things like homeless people in the streets, I'm a Democrat."

He was thinking about that in his Pocono hotel, sitting there late as the TV rumbled on—but he was also thinking about the car. Their mediocre showing in Daytona was disturbing. Their motor and chassis setups were fine, and they hadn't lost any time in the pits. Nevertheless, the car was slow, and they were beginning to suspect that they understood the problem. The Pontiac Grand Prix was a smaller car than its chief competitors, the Ford Thunderbird and Chevrolet Lumina—and the most important difference was the rear deck lid, the trunk in the showroom version of the car. Because it was smaller, there were fewer square inches for a downforce of air to keep the car steady as it cut through the wind. On smaller tracks, it was less of a problem; the key things there were horsepower and handling. But on tracks that were more than a mile and a half, there was nothing more important than aerodynamics. In the past, their problems could be overcome—a little creative fudging here and there. Now with Gary Nelson as NASCAR's inspector, the rules were enforced more strictly and the Pontiac teams felt pinned to the wall.

Pocono, however, was a different kind of track. It was huge—two miles around—but flat in the turns, which cut the raw speed. Kyle thought they might be able to compensate: with John Wilson's motors and Robin's ability to set up the chassis, there was really no reason why they couldn't be competitive. Thinking about it in his motel room, while politics flickered across the television screen, he was eager to get the car on the track. But the weather on Friday had not been a friend. The fog was so thick you couldn't see a thing, and it lingered all day. Saturday was better. The fog finally lifted, but on the first lap of practice the gear-shifter broke on Petty's Pontiac—"a minor anxiety attack," said Robin. It took a while to fix it, and then some time for tinkering with the chassis, but by the late morning practice, they were running pretty fast. Bob Romano, timing the best cars with a hand-held watch, reported that Kyle was in the top five—with an outside shot at winning the pole. Petty, however, hit the curb on his qualifying lap, which cost him some time, and he ended up qualifying 13th.

Race day came with unanswered questions, and Robin was tight—worried, he said, about the shifter. Kyle, on the other hand, seemed loose. He was sitting on a generator in front of the truck, swapping stories with his amiable tire man, Glenn Funderburke, when a swarm of autograph seekers descended. There were at least fifty of them, armed with caps and posters and a sweatshirt or two, even a cardboard box they wanted him to sign. Petty got up and did his duty, standing there smiling in his neatly creased jeans and blue shirt buttoned all the way to the collar. In a way, it was distracting just before a race, but it was an expectation that went with the sport—one, in fact, that his father encouraged—and the only way around it was to hide in the truck. Petty preferred to grin and bear it. Most of the fans were friendly enough, and they were, after all, the cornerstone of the sport.

After awhile, the crowd began to thin and he ducked in the truck to dress for the race. He was ready now, eager to see what the car would do, and a half hour later when the green flag fell, he could tell right away that the setup was good. Within a couple of laps, he was moving through the field, and by lap 14, he was in 10th place and gaining on his father who was then running 9th. Richard Petty had qualified well, starting the race in 7th position, but now, as usual, he was beginning to fade. Someone said it was like watching Willie Mays in his last year with the Giants, his heart still strong but his reflexes gone. Whatever the analogy, the King of racing was no longer a threat, and Kyle passed him easily on lap 17.

Within a few more laps, he was all the way to 4th, drafting with Kulwicki and Ernie Irvan to try to catch the leader, Davey Allison. So far, although Allison was in a class by itself, leading the field by twenty-five lengths, both Kyle and Kulwicki were chipping away, punching a hole in the air together and gaining by as much as a half second a lap. The lead was smaller by the next pit stop, and Kyle's crew were fast—changing four tires in less than twenty seconds, which moved him momentarily into second position.

"Great stop, guys," he said.

"The least we can do," said John Wilson calmly.

Allison was still the leader of the race, and after a few laps Kulwicki and Sterling Marlin were gaining quickly on Petty from behind. As the race wore on, those three cars were clearly faster, but Kyle and the crew were hanging in there—and after another perfect pit stop, he took the lead on lap 120. The moment didn't last. Allison passed him within three laps, and then Kulwicki. It was hard to know what to think at this point. There was nothing they could do to make the car go faster. The setup was perfect, and the guys in the pit had never been better. But when they pitted again with sixty laps to go, he knew there were cars that he couldn't outrun.

Then came a moment of elemental horror.

Davey Allison stalled coming out of the pit, and by the time he got his car running again, he had fallen from first to seventh on the track. He began to weave his way through the traffic, back to sixth, then fifth, then past Darrell Waltrip to move up to fourth. Waltrip, however, was not giving up. His car was fast and on the 149th lap of the race he drove low on the backstretch to try to pass Davey.

Allison cut down at an angle to block him, and when he did, he clipped the front of Waltrip's Chevrolet. The contact was slight and accidental, and Waltrip was essentially uneffected by it. Davey, however, began sliding to his left, and just as his wheels hit the infield grass, his car took flight. Kyle could see it soaring past him, the roof pointed down, before it landed hood-first in a violent flip.

It was barrel-rolling now—eleven times in the next four seconds—with pieces of sheet metal flying everywhere: the hood, the roof, the right-front tire, all ripping loose as if a bomb had exploded inside. It finally stopped, top-down—and it was impossible to tell, in the first few seconds, whether or not there was life inside.

"That was a bad wreck right there," Kyle told his crew, and his voice was stricken. Within a few minutes, though, the good news came: Allison survived. He had a broken collarbone and arm, broken bones in his wrist, but there seemed to be nothing that couldn't be fixed. Still, it was clear that his season was changed. Allison had led in the points all year, and he had the strongest car before the wreck. Now, who knew? It would obviously be awhile before he could race at full strength, and his championship run was now in doubt. Kyle felt bad that those things happened, but he couldn't stop to think about it now. He had a race to finish, and he thought he was still in a position to win it. He was slower than Kulwicki and one or two others, but the fastest car didn't always prevail. He had learned that much in his racing career.

He was in fifth place after the race restarted, but the laps ticked away and he couldn't move up. In fact, the other cars were pulling away, and there seemed to be nothing he could do about it. "Kyle Petty's Pontiac is not responding," said Eli Gold of MRN. He was still in 5th place when they pitted for gas—still trailing Kulwicki, Rudd, Mark Martin, and Ted Musgrave. However, when he returned to the track, he had fallen to 7th. Darrell Waltrip and Harry Gant, who had run only intermittently with the leaders, had not yet pitted for the splash of gas that everybody else had to have to finish. Waltrip and Gant were famous for that—so smooth on the track that they could stretch gas further than anybody else and occasionally win races that should have been out of reach. Now they were about to do it again. Waltrip was first, Gant was second, and with five laps to go it was clear that neither intended to stop. Everybody in the pits kept waiting: Surely, this time they would run out of gas. But neither did, and Waltrip won the race with Gant just behind him.

Kyle was 7th and angry about it. Waltrip and Gant were frustrating enough, but he was also deeply disillusioned with his car. They had struggled in Daytona, but not this time. They had had a perfect chassis setup, their pit stops were superb, and although he didn't want to talk about it, he knew he had driven an outstanding race. What more could they do? If that was the best they could get from a Pontiac, the rest of the season didn't look very promising.

"We ought to send 'em to the crusher," he muttered.

At the moment at least, that's how he felt.

*　*　*

The first thing Monday morning, Felix Sabates was on the phone. He called Bill France in Daytona Beach, and told him something had to be done. Felix had cultivated a relationship with France, the president of NASCAR, taking him for rides on his magnificent yacht, a 112-foot Hatteras he had named *Victory Lane*. They would spend hours on the deck, talking philosophically about the future of the sport, France sipping Scotch from an ice tea glass. Over the years, they had come to respect each other's judgment, and on July 20, the day after Pocono, Sabates put the case as plainly as he could. The Pontiac Grand Prix was a splendid car with a long, rich history in the sport of racing, but under Gary Nelson's rules it was no longer competitive. Something had to give or the Pontiac teams, including his own, would have to start thinking about switching to Ford.

Felix felt sure that France was listening. He had never found him to be unreasonable—and within a few hours Gary Nelson called. "How wide were you guys in Daytona?" he asked Robin Pemberton.

"I don't know," said Robin. "You made us cut back."

Actually, Robin knew the dimensions exactly. Their rear bumper width was 63 and ⅞ inches until the NASCAR inspectors made them cut to 61. For Grand Prixs, 61 was stock—but when the Petty team shaved the car to that width, the aerodynamics no longer worked.

Nelson told Robin they could widen it back to 63 and ⅞, still not as wide as the bumper of a Ford, though it sounded like a fairly helpful concession. In fact, Robin had already done it. Before Pocono, he had decided that they simply wouldn't race at 61—not voluntarily. They would widen the bumper, and if NASCAR caught them they would cut it again.

The good news was that after Nelson's phone call, they wouldn't have to play that game of cat and mouse. The bad news was that Nelson merely gave them what they were already running—and at Pocono it hadn't been enough.

Morale at that point was beginning to falter. It was hard on the team to take a car to Talladega, the next race on the schedule, knowing that they probably didn't have a chance to win. Talladega was the biggest, fastest oval track on the circuit, a place where the aerodynamics were critical. It was disheartening to think of all the progress they had made—stronger engines, faster pitstops, dramatic improvements in the chassis setups—and still feel crippled by the shape of the car.

The situation brought other tensions to the surface. Some of the guys were complaining, for example, that Robin played favorites in the way he ran the team. He relied most heavily on Jim Long and John Wilson, while some of the others felt like the B-team. There was a lot of grumbling over dinner when they got to Talladega, but Richard Bostic said it would pass. Bostic, the truck driver, had felt the sting of Robin's wrath on occasion—especially in Daytona when there had been a misunderstanding over gears—but he said all that was part of the game.

"When you've been around it as long as I have . . . " he said, but then he let that thought trail off, and substituted another in its place.

"What we really need is a win."

The practice sessions looked pretty good. They were drafting well with the fastest cars, and when they qualified on Friday afternoon, they came in 6th—even though the engine got hot on the second lap and may have cost them a little bit of time.

"That's about right," said Robin before the race. "I think we're about a 6th-place car."

On the morning of the race, it was threatening rain. Clouds were hovering near the Georgia line, a low, gray mass above the first bluffs of the mountains. As the morning wore on, it grew sunny and hot, typical of Talladega in the summer. The track was nestled on the floor of a valley, and legend had it that the area was cursed—having served at one time as a burial ground for the Indians whose spirits still roamed when they were annoyed. Driver Tiny Lund was killed in Talladega, Kyle himself didn't miss it by much, and back in 1973, the great Bobby Isaac dropped out of a race even though his car was running just fine. He said a voice had told him to quit.

For the majority of the Winston Cup drivers, however, the most mysterious thing about Talladega was the draft—why it worked better for some cars than others. Kyle, for example, could draft with anybody in practice, keeping up with Kulwicki or anyone else, unless he happened to be last in line. In that case the others would drive off and leave him. It had happened time and time again, and he knew it was critical when the race got started to make sure somebody else was behind him.

Of course, that was easier said than done, but the race started well. Petty moved up to 5th on the first time around, and after two laps he passed his father and Davey Allison to move up to 3rd. It was incredible that Davey was in the car. He had plates in his arm and pins in his wrist from the wreck in Pocono, and had been in a hospital bed until Friday. But according to the rules of Winston Cup racing, he had to start the race and complete at least a lap if he wanted to win points in the season's competition. After that, he could turn the car over to his relief driver, Bobby Hillin.

Everybody knew that the rule was dangerous. What if Davey got caught in another wreck? What kind of permanent damage could it do? A lot of drivers, including Richard Petty who once had to race with a broken neck, were lobbying for a change. But NASCAR held firm, and race after race the drivers felt compelled to take silly chances. Ernie Irvan had climbed into the car a day after breaking his collarbone in Atlanta. Ken Schrader had been racing with a herniated disc. Some of it was a matter of competitiveness and pride, but it was also a capitulation to the rules.

Fortunately for Davey, a rain cloud drifted in from the west and drops began to fall on the fifth lap of the race. NASCAR called a caution and Davey pitted to give way to Bobby Hillin. This time at least, there was no harm done.

The race restarted on lap 11 with Ricky Rudd in the lead and Sterling Marlin 2nd. Kyle was 3rd with Dale Jarrett 4th, and within a lap the top four cars were pulling away. But after five laps a second group of cars, led by the Ford of Geoff Bodine, caught up with the first. Suddenly, there was a furious battle for position. Kyle lost a spot to Jarrett, and once out of line, fell two more positions to 6th. He gained a spot when Sterling Marlin also was caught out of line—and then the battle ended, as the cars settled back into single file.

That's the way it went in Talladega—desperate pitched battles for position here and there, punctuated by long and relatively uneventful stretches with the cars hooked up in long freight trains. Kyle was 5th in this particular train, and that's where he stayed for the next thirty laps, until the leaders pitted on lap 51. Once again, his crew was fast, and when he returned to the track he was back up to third.

"Great stop, guys," he said.

It was getting to be a habit, this splendid work by the guys in the pit, but Petty didn't have much time to enjoy it. He was somewhere in the middle of a group of seven cars—the top 5 in the race and two that were lapped but still pretty fast. Ricky Rudd and Sterling Marlin were low on the track, while Kyle was caught in a slower high groove. The battle for position raged for ten laps before the cars were sorted into single file. Rudd was in front, and after losing a couple of spots trying to pass, Kyle was at the end of the string of seven. Steve Knipe was telling him to stay in line, but he could feel himself beginning to lose the draft. "I've got to have somebody behind me," he said, and he made a desperate pass inside of Elliott.

This time he made it and the pattern continued for a large part of the race—Kyle in a battle with the five or six fastest cars. Even when he pitted and lost position on the track, he made his way back easily to the top 6 or 7. All in all he was feeling strong, but his spirits fell on lap 89. He was running 5th behind Marlin, Elliott, Ernie Irvan, and Hillin, and they began to break away from the rest of the field. For a lap or two he held his ground, but with no one behind him he could feel himself losing his grip on the draft. He was two lengths back, then three, then four.

"They're breaking away from me, man," he said.

"I know," said Robin. "Do the best you can do."

Within three laps, Kyle was twenty lengths back, and the hard truth was, it would get even worse. There was a string of three cars gaining on him from behind. They caught him quickly, and blew right by and five more cars were now bearing down. Before he knew it, he was running 13th—and he was still at the end of a long string of cars. He was trying desperately to pass Dale Jarrett, who was battling hard to hold on to the 12th spot. "I ought to slam the son of a bitch," said Petty, and there was an edge of desperation in his voice.

Robin shook his head. They had been through some frustrating times this season—missing the setup in Rockingham and Richmond, wrecking the car in four other places—but seldom on any of those occasions had Kyle come close to losing his cool. Now he was fuming, saying things that he wouldn't ordinarily, but the good news was, he was not giving up. He battled his way around Dale Jarrett, and he was moving up again with other cars behind him. Quickly now, he made up ground—made it as high as fourth at one point, but with ten laps to go Bill Elliott and Ricky Rudd were able to draft past him, and Michael Waltrip was bearing down in a hurry.

He was racing now to hold on to 6th place—Waltrip on his bumper as the laps ticked away. "He's looking high," warned Steve Knipe, but Kyle slid up the track to block him. "Now low"—and Kyle cut down.

He managed to hold on for a 6th place finish, and when his voice came on the radio it was calm. "We had a hell of a motor and a hell of a crew," he said. "You guys were great."

Still, they were worried about the car, and when they had a week off and went to test for the next race at Watkins Glen, Robin was determined to make some improvements. The test, at first, did not go well. Their times were slow on the hilly road course—an 11-turn track where they raced clockwise—until Robin was struck with a simple idea. If they couldn't do much with the rear of the car, why not try to compensate with the front?

If they could make a few changes in the lines here and there—nothing so blatant that they couldn't pass inspection—they might improve the way they cut through the air. They got some tape and pieces of foam and some strips of cardboard they cut from a box. They taped the cardboard and foam on the nose, making it wider in a few key places, and amazingly enough it seemed to work. The car was faster on the next several laps—so much faster that at first they were stunned. They tested some more, and the car was still fast and they decided it was time to make the changes permanent. They returned to Charlotte as quickly as they could, and the guys in the fabrication shop went to work. Robin left it with them—Jim Sutton, Len Sherrill and all the rest. If there had been some grousing on the team before, people feeling like they were second-string this was a way to refute that notion. "It's up to you guys," Robin told them. "You're the ones who can make the car fast." Which is what they did. They cut the old nose off and built a new one precisely in the shape of the cardboard and foam—and when they took the car to practice before the race, they were delighted once again by the way it performed.

They were one of the fastest—and in the run for the pole on Friday afternoon, Petty's speed once again was impressive: 116.416. It was nowhere near a record for the track, but it was the fastest speed of the day so far, and it kept holding up. Ernie Irvan, Ricky Rudd, Rusty Wallace—all of them were slower and they were the undisputed aces of the road course tracks.

Back at the truck, Petty was getting nervous. He had never won a road course pole, and Jane Gossage could tell he wanted it badly. Jane is the PR representative for the team, and there are few people better at reading Petty's moods. He didn't say much, but Jane could tell that his hopes were rising as one by one the good drivers fell short—Mark Martin, Bill Elliott, Brett Bodine.

As they neared the end of the qualifying round, only Dale Earnhardt was left to disappoint him—and at least in practice he hadn't come close. Out on the track this time he was fast, hurtling his way through string of S-turns and the hairpin reverse at the end of the backstretch. When the run was over he was on the pole, and Petty was left with what might have been.

"It's the first time I've ever seen him hang his head," Jane said later. "He really wanted to establish himself as a road course driver."

Winning the pole would have helped do that. Coming in second probably would not. But Jane Gossage smiled. The thing to do now was win the race.

Race day came with a drizzling rain, as gray as the memories that hovered at the track. The year before on the fifth lap of the race, the veteran J. D. McDuffie was killed. He was coming into turn 5, which is almost a U at the end of the backstretch—a dangerous spot, as race officials had every reason to know. In the days just before McDuffie was killed, six drivers had wrecked at the turn in practice, including Michael Waltrip who broke his shoulder. The backstretch was the fastest place on the track, with speeds of 175 m.p.h., and you had to hit the brakes hard coming into the turn. But something broke when McDuffie got there, and his car went skidding in a cloud of smoke—sliding across a patch of grass and slamming into a barrier of cable and tires. It flipped and landed on the roof, and everybody knew that it had to be bad. Driver Jimmy Means got there first. He had wrecked behind McDuffie, also sliding across the grass, but he was unhurt and rushed immediately to McDuffie's car. "J.D.," he called—but there was no response. Means, a decent, soft-spoken man, began waving frantically for help, but when the ambulance and paramedics arrived, there was nothing they could do. McDuffie's skull was fractured. He was already dead.

It was a shocking moment, for death is rare in Winston Cup racing. McDuffie was the twenty fourth driver at that level of the sport to die on the track since the founding of NASCAR in the 1940s. Eight drivers died in the 1950s, seven in the sixties, and four each in the seventies and eighties. McDuffie was the first in the 1990s, and he had been one of the most popular drivers in the sport—a throwback of sorts to the days when racing was a poor man's passion. J.D. was fifty-two when he died, a sharecropper's son who never had a lot of formal education and gave up life as a factory worker and hired-hand mechanic to drive his own car.

There was a pride that went with his new independence; as one writer put it, "behind the wheel he was a man, not a cog," and within a few years he was a dirt track champion. He graduated to Winston Cup, where he started 653 races and never won—never had a big sponsorship or the kind of money that made winning possible. He had had his moments—more than 100 top 10 finishes, a dozen top 5s and that glorious afternoon at Dover Downs when he won the pole for the Delaware 500. It was back in 1978, and nobody could take the achievement away. At least for that lap, his Pontiac was the fastest thing on the track.

Ten years later, McDuffie was nearly killed. His car caught fire in a wreck in Daytona and badly burned his leg, face and hands. A few hours later, his wife, Ima Jean, was standing quietly by his hospital bed.

"J.D.," she said, "don't you think this is about enough?"

"No," he said, and his voice was firm.

"J.D.," she insisted, "I wish you wouldn't build another car."

"I got to," he said, and that was that.

Lynda Petty had lived with the same compulsion, had seen her own husband and son nearly killed, and when J.D. died at Watkins Glen, she picked up the phone and called Ima Jean. They talked for awhile, but in the end there was nothing she could say. J.D. died doing what he loved. There was a measure of consolation in that, but there was also the memory of the fatal wreck. Ima Jean saw it on television—the Pontiac sliding across the grass and flipping wildly across the barrier of tires.

"Oh Lord," she cried. "That was J.D."

Before the next race in Watkins Glenn, Ima Jean filed a suit in federal court. She contended that NASCAR and the operators of the track had been irresponsible, refusing to correct what they knew was a hazard. She asked for $4.25 million.

The suit and the memories hung over the sport, but when Sunday came nobody talked about them much. In the hours leading up to the start of a race, the last thing they wanted to talk about was death.

In Kyle Petty's truck, they were talking about a win. Not that anybody was superstitious about it, but earlier that morning coming into the track Big John Youk found a four-leaf clover. He picked it tenderly and put it in his wallet, and a couple of hours later he showed it to a friend. "I've just got a feeling," Big John said.

Richard Bostic had it too. He was talking to a reporter who was hanging near the truck, and he offered a prediction he hadn't made all year. "We're gonna win," he said.

For Bostic, it was more than just a hunch. He could see all the pieces falling into place—the car running fast, the morale of the team picking up accordingly. And they also had a little surprise. Back at the shop, Mike Ford, who handled the jack during the team's pit stops, had come to Robin with a novel idea. Pitting, he said, was always slower at Watkins Glen because the cars were racing in a clockwise direction, opposite from the way they raced all year. They pitted in the opposite direction too, and most teams' rhythms were disrupted by that—changing the left tires first, instead of the right. Mike Ford suggested they start with the right. Robin wasn't sure it would make any difference, but he was intrigued by his jackman's spirit of innovation. He said they could try it a few times at the shop, and when they did the results were astonishing: four tire changes in seventeen seconds, more than two seconds faster than the best stop of the year. If they could come even close to that in the race, they would gain an unbelievable advantage.

"Hell," said Robin, "let's go for it."

Race day came with a round of jitters—the jitters of excitement rather than doubt. It also came with frustrating weather, a gray mist falling as the race was set to start. There was nothing to do but sit and wait, until the rain finally quit around 3 P.M. It took another hour to dry the track, and the race didn't start until after 4:30.

When it did, Petty was fast. He was running second going into turn 1, a sharp, narrow right at the bottom of a hill. For the first eight laps he was chasing the leader, Dale Earnhardt, and the two of them were pulling away from the field. About that time they saw Ernie Irvan coming. He was flying through the S's and the back straightaway, passing Ricky Rudd and other fast cars and now taking aim on Earnhardt and Petty. He blew past Kyle at the end of the lap, and two laps later he took the lead.

It was only the beginning of a seesaw battle. On lap 11, Petty passed Earnhardt coming into turn 1, and slowly began to cut into the lead. He was eight lengths behind Ernie on lap 14, five lengths back the next time around. On lap 17, he decided to pit—the first car to do it—and the stop went poorly. Mike Ford slipped as he circled the car, which cost them some time, and the stop lasted more than twenty-three seconds.

A caution flag fell as they returned to the track. Todd Bodine went skidding across the grass, and his car slammed hard into a barrier of tires. Ordinarily, it would have been a disaster—not only for Bodine, but for Petty as well. On an oval track, a green-flag pit stop will cost you a lap. You get it back when your rivals pit, but if a caution comes out to slow the pace, they can change four tires before a lap is completed. You lose a lap, your rivals don't. It's the most hated twist of luck in racing.

On a road course, however, everything is different. It takes nearly a minute and eighteen seconds to cover the 2.428 miles at Watkins Glen—which is more than enough time to change four tires. Petty could pit without losing a lap, and when the caution came out he could stay on the track while everybody else rushed in for new tires. Through a stroke of pure luck, he was leading the race.

But could he hold it?

When the green flag dropped on lap 21, it was easy to see that the two fastest cars were Petty and Irvan. For the next four laps they pulled away from the field, racing almost nose to tail. On lap 25, Ernie took the lead, passing low on the hill as they entered turn 1. But Kyle kept chasing, running no more than five lengths back, and on lap 36 he made his move. He stood on the gas as they hit the backstretch, and almost before Irvan saw him coming, they were two abreast going into the loop—a rapid sequence of four sharp turns: right-left-left-right.

If they stayed two abreast somebody would wreck. Petty had the angle and showed no signs of backing off—and for an agonizing moment neither did Ernie. Their speeds were approaching 170, and still neither driver had hit the brakes. Common sense took hold at the last possible second: Ernie slowed down and pulled in behind.

On lap 38, a caution came out, and everybody headed immediately for the pits—the new battleground to see who would lead. This time Petty's crew was fast, and Kyle was easily the first car out. Robin was ecstatic. "Way to do it, boys," he said. "Way to kick some ass."

Suddenly, however, he saw they had a problem. Raindrops were beginning to fall on the track, and Kyle was not the leader of the race. Dick Trickle was. He hadn't had a competitive car all day; in fact, he had lost control and spun—but when the caution came out he stayed on the track. His strategy was simple. They had five laps to go before the halfway point, and if they could make it that far the race was official. With the rain falling harder and darkness coming on, it was possible that the day would end under caution. As the leader at that point, Trickle would win.

"Son of a bitch," said Robin. "Some people have the luck."

The gods, however, had a different idea. The rains let up on lap 43, and NASCAR decided to restart the race. Kyle passed Trickle in the first hundred feet and immediately began to pull away by himself. Ernie had been 5th coming out of the pits, which meant he had at least four cars to pass. Two laps later at the halfway point, Kyle was cruising well ahead of the field, as the skies once again began to open up. The caution came out with Ernie racing frantically to try to catch up. He nearly wrecked as he hit a wet spot, and wound up 3rd when the caution took effect. The drizzle was all around them now, soaking the track, and after a few more laps, NASCAR decided it was time to park. Even if the rain were to quit right away, there wouldn't be time to dry the track before dark.

Kyle had trouble believing it at first. He stepped out of the car looking tense and unsure, as a crew from ESPN approached. When the official word came that he had won, he said he was lucky and cut his eyes toward the sky. The guys on the team were less restrained. It had been a long time coming—this first victory of the year for the Mello Yello crew, but now they were happy and ready for more.

Jane Gossage grinned when somebody mentioned the psychic she had hired in May. The fortune-teller predicted a second-place finish for Kyle in the Winston, which he got. She also predicted he would win two races, which meant he still had one more to go. For Robin, however, the most important prophecy was his own. Earlier in the year, when the team was mired around 20th in the points, he had made this prediction:

If they could make the top ten by Watkins Glen, they could make the top 5 by the end of the year.

They were now up to 9th, and slowly but surely they were starting to believe.

PART THREE

THE CHAMPIONSHIP RACE

CHAPTER 10

MOVING UP

Almost from the moment he touched down in Michigan, Kyle Petty could tell that something was wrong. His friend, Jane Gossage, met him at the plane, and though her emotions were under control he could see a different look in her eyes. Petty had come to Michigan feeling loose, still savoring his win at Watkins Glen and hoping to prove it was more than just luck—more that the fruits of a well-timed rain. But he forgot all that when Jane broke the news. Clifford Allison, she said, was dead. The younger brother of Davey, a part-time driver on the Busch Grand National Circuit, one level down from Winston Cup, had been killed in practice at the Michigan Speedway.

Kyle had trouble believing it at first. How much tragedy could one family stand? He asked how it happened, and Jane told him what she knew: It was a one-car wreck, Clifford hit the wall. Kyle shook his head and walked away and then came back and asked more questions. Jane thought later he was trying to digest it a piece at a time, and she wondered what memories were flooding through his mind—the football games in the Talladega infield, the bicycle chases around the asphalt banks; memories of boys growing up at the track. Kyle said later the memories were part of it, but he was actually thinking more of Clifford's parents. He felt great affection for Bobby and Judy Allison. After his wreck in Talladega, when he was lying in a hospital bed in Birmingham, and fever and infection were racing through his body, the Allisons came every day to see him. Kyle was touched by that. Bobby had been such a rival of his father's, and once in a while on the track it had been nasty. Time had long since healed those wounds, and now they were part of the same large family—the same community of small-town nomads who spent more time at the track than at home. The men, of course, had made that choice. But the women had not—the wives and mothers and sisters and daughters . . . they were merely playing the hand they were dealt, and in the case of the Allisons the hand had been cruel.

The death of Clifford was the worst, of course, but there had been so much that came before it. In 1988, Bobby barely survived a wreck in Pocono. He cut a tire and got t-boned by a slower car, and for days he was hanging pretty close to death. Even now, more than four years later, he wore an equilibrium patch behind his ear, and still couldn't remember much from that year. Even earlier, his brother Donnie was nearly killed in Charlotte, and then of course there was Davey this year—his terrifying wreck with Kyle in Charlotte, where he hit the wall at 180 and had to be helicoptered away; and then Pocono—the TV image of his car flipping wildly and flying apart. Kyle tried to imagine the emotions of Judy Allison. How could any mother stand up to this?

He wasn't alone in asking that question. Down in Hueytown, Alabama, the Allisons' home, friends began to gather at the Iceberg Restaurant. It was a favorite eating place of the Allisons, and the people came and wept and worried about Judy. "I doubt she's handling it," said the Iceberg's owner, Gay Ann McCrary. "When Davey got his arm hurt, she was pitiful. She's crazy about those children. She said every time they got in a race car, it just tore her apart."

Kyle knew Bobby was different in a way. He was a driver and

he understood the risks, but you couldn't help but worry about his burden too. Bobby was there when the accident happened. He told Liz Clarke of the *Charlotte Observer* that he was standing in the pits near Clifford's crew chief, Barry Owens, when he heard Owens say in a frustrated voice: "He just crashed." Bobby saw the ambulance leaving pit road, and turned toward Owens. "Barry," he said, "is he talking to you?" Owens shook his head and called the car on the radio again. There was nothing. Bobby started walking now, not running, but heading toward the car at a rapid clip. A few seconds later a NASCAR inspector tried to stop him. "They don't want you up there," the inspector said. But Allison kept going. He could see Clifford slumped to the right in the seat and Gary Nelson leaning through the window. The NASCAR inspectors tried to stop him again, but Bobby pushed past. "I will not get in anybody's way," he said.

He had a clear view now from the front of the car, and suddenly he could see that his son was dead. There were no visible marks but Bobby knew. About that time, he saw Elisa, Clifford's young wife, rushing toward the car. He reached out to stop her.

"Is he talking?" Elisa demanded.

"No," said Bobby.

"Is he breathing?"

"I don't know."

In the hours and days that followed Clifford's death, Kyle wrote his condolences to the Allison family, and said a few prayers for Judy and the others, but like every driver on the Winston Cup circuit, he also had a defense mechanism. It was the view, essentially, that something odd must have happened, something freaky. Maybe the victim forgot to buckle up, or maybe his equipment was old and didn't work, but whatever went wrong, it was not the kind of thing that happened to good teams—not to teams like his own, where the people and equipment were always the best. *It couldn't be me*: That was every driver's bottom line, and careers ended quickly with the first hint of doubt.

Somewhere in his mind, Petty understood. He knew it was an elaborate rationalization—maybe even a desperate case of self-deception. Nevertheless, he believed it. Otherwise, how could he get in the car?

*   *   *

Clifford's funeral was not until Monday. In between, the drivers had to race. On Friday, they came to the track to qualify, and Davey Allison was right there with them. Some people talked about his courage; others whispered that he was being self-centered. How could he do such a thing to his mother? Kyle thought the issue was really quite clear. After his wreck in Pocono, Davey had said: "It's hard, but this is my life." Kyle knew Davey had to get on with it.

As always, Davey's car was fast. He qualified 3rd while Kyle was 15th, but the Petty team was confident about the race. In practice, they were one of the top 5 cars, and Robin thought they were better than when they came to Michigan in June. Kyle had finished that race 4th.

Sunday arrived with beautiful weather, a pale blue sky and 75 degrees, and one hundred thousand people in the stands. The green flag fell just after noon, and once again Petty started well. He was passing cars for the first five laps, and had moved up to 9th when there was an ugly wreck in the turn just behind him. Bobby Hamilton started spinning to his right and Geoff Bodine, who was a car length behind, had to hit the brakes. Bodine missed Hamilton but went spinning toward the wall, and with his car sliding backward, he collided almost head-on with Greg Sacks. Sacks bit his tongue. The other two drivers appeared to be all right, but the wreck set the tone for the first half of the race. There were crashes, on the average, every twenty laps, and several of them looked pretty bad. Ricky Rudd hit the wall on lap 56; a gas line broke and a stream of fire chased his car up the track. A few laps later, Lake Speed wrecked and there was a whoosh of flame from under his hood, engulfing the whole right side of the car. Speed headed straight for the grass and jumped, not even waiting for the car to stop.

Petty, through it all, remained unscathed. He was now in 8th place and gaining in a hurry—passing Brett Bodine for 7th and then Davey Allison and Darrell Waltrip. For the next two laps he battled with Kulwicki, running side by side in the turns and down the front stretch at 195 m.p.h. Kyle finally passed him low on the track, and three laps later he caught Sterling Marlin. He was now in 3rd place and closing in quickly on Bill Elliott and Ernie Irvan. Elliott was leading, with Irvan on his bumper, and with Petty coming on, it was suddenly a three-car race for the lead. Petty made it to 2nd, as he and Irvan both got around Elliott—but Petty's tires were wearing and he was low on gas. On lap 134, he decided to pit.

The stop went fine, but when he returned to the track there was cause for alarm—a whole new twist in the drama of the race. One by one the fast cars pitted—Kyle and Davey, Elliott and Irvan, Kulwicki and Waltrip; really the whole field except for one car: the dreaded Oldsmobile of Harry Gant. Nobody worried that Gant was fast. In 1992 at least, he was most often the tortoise of the NASCAR world, poking along and staying out of trouble. He was also *the* grand master at stretching his fuel—better at it even than Darrell Waltrip—and his strategy this time was to win the race by pitting fewer times. He had already done it at Dover Downs, and now he was about to pull it off again. Gant didn't pit until lap 150, which meant he could make it without another stop—and nobody else was in that position. For Petty and the others, there was only one hope: something had to happen to cause a caution, but the laps rolled by and nothing did. A race that had once been littered with wrecks was now becoming smooth and uneventful.

Petty, meanwhile, was beginning to fade—nothing serious, but his Pontiac was tight on a new set of tires, and he was now running 5th in the fastest group of cars. With twenty laps to go, the leaders started pitting—just a splash of gas for most—but Harry Gant kept right on cruising. His car sputtered slightly on the final lap, but coasted across the finish line for the win.

Petty was frustrated. He knew that Gant was a popular driver—an unassuming veteran from the town of Taylorsville, North Carolina He was only a couple of years younger than Richard Petty, and at the age of fifty-two he was trying to win races anyway he could. Still, his tactics cost Kyle a top 5 finish. Petty was 6th and angry about it, and he let himself vent his frustrations in print. "We had a top 5 car today," he said, "but finished 6th because somebody was conducting a mileage test. . . . It's not fair to us, and it's not fair to the fans."

The statement was out of character for Petty—not a very gracious ending to the day, and the lapse was all the more curious because of what they accomplished. Kyle jumped from 9th to 6th in the points, and was now within striking distance of 5th. In his thirteen years as a driver, he had never finished the season any higher than 7th. Whatever his frustrations with Harry Gant, he was now within range of his best year ever. There were ten races left . . . no time now to be looking back.

The next stop was Bristol, and everybody knew it would be an event. The track was the steepest anywhere in NASCAR and by far the fastest of any its size. Now it also appeared to be the roughest. Vibrations were so bad in the last week of testing that it was hard for the drivers to focus their eyes. "My brain is shaking," reported Ernie Irvan, and almost every driver agreed.

The problems came mostly from a new coat of pavement—concrete this time, instead of asphalt—which officials had installed with the best of intentions. At the race in April, the tires had chewed the asphalt to gravel, especially in the turns, and Petty was one of those who wrecked. He hit a loose patch coming out of turn 4, and his car slid suddenly into the wall. Track officials decided to try a harder surface, but the turns were too steep, and the concrete tended to dry in ripples.

To make matters worse for Petty and his team, the car was running slow in practice, and nothing they did to it seemed to help. They tried new springs, new gears, a spring rubber in the rear. They bolted chunks of lead to the frame to redistribute the weight, and still the speeds didn't get any better. The car was handling well enough in the turns, which was always critically important in the race, but qualifying would be another matter. In a test of pure speed, with only one car on the track at a time, Robin had a feeling that they might be embarrassed.

Robin was right. Twenty-five cars were faster than Petty's, which meant he would start the race near the rear. Even worse, only eighteen cars could pit on the front stretch, and it was a disadvantage to pit on the back. During a caution, when speeds were slow, your rivals could pit and change four tires before you even made it around to your pit. Too many races had been lost for that reason.

Robin thought about qualifying again. They had that option. In the second round of qualifying, cars that didn't make the top 15 were given a chance to improve on their times. The three fastest

A fog hovers over the track in Daytona.

A pensive
moment for
Robin
Pemberton,
Kyle's crew
chief.

Bill Elliott, a contender for the championship.

Geoff Bodine times his rivals during qualifying at Rockingham.

FACING PAGE: Dale Earnhardt and Kyle Petty battle down the backstretch at North Wilkesboro.

Alan Kulwicki on the hood of his car after winning the 1992 Winston Cup championship. Early the next year, Kulwicki was killed . . . in a plane crash outside of Bristol.

Darrell Waltrip, the winningest driver on the circuit after the retirement of Richard Petty.

Davey Allison, whose season was a mixture of heartbreak and triumph.

Ricky Rudd, deep in thought just before qualifying.

Dale Earnhardt between practice
sessions at Martinsville.

Brett Bodine waits his turn to
qualify.

Davey Allison—still wearing a flak vest to protect injured ribs from an earlier crash—walks away after hitting the wall in Martinsville.

Filling gas cans before the race at Darlington.

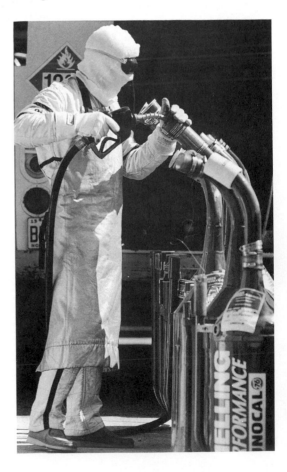

cars in the consolation round could still win the right to pit on the front. Conventional wisdom said you had to go for it, but Robin said no. For one thing, cars were wrecking like crazy in practice— Richard Petty, Michael Waltrip, Bill Elliott and others—and Robin didn't want to take that chance. More than that, it was simply a matter of respect for his driver. They had done everything they could with the car, and the only way now to find more speed would be to ask Petty to push a little harder.

"I'm not going to do it," said Robin. "When it comes to qualifying, Kyle is a finesse driver, not a kamikaze. He knows where the car needs to be on the track. I am not going to ask him to drive any different."

It was the kind of decision that set Robin apart—an understanding of the foibles of his driver that the greatest crew chiefs had to have. If Petty was, by his own admission, better in a race than he was in qualifying, then it was not Robin's place to try to change him. It was a question of trust—which was far too important, and far too fragile in a sport this intense. Robin thought Kyle would be fine in the race, precisely because he had such a feel for the car. And despite its limitations when it came to raw speed, Robin thought the car would be fine too.

"It's got the look," he said. "When it's time to race, we'll be okay."

The green flag fell and Robin was a prophet. Petty was moving up quickly through the field, which had become his habit, and he never looked better than he did in Bristol. The August race was always at night, and the floodlights danced and glittered off the cars. The Mello Yello Pontiac was made for these nights—splashes of yellow and green and red against a field of black. "That forty-two car is looking sweet," said Felix Sabates.

Petty passed four cars in the first eight laps, and was gaining on a fifth when the leader, Ernie Irvan, went spinning in the turn. Nobody touched him, but he lost control and went crashing backward toward the wall near the pits. Irvan wasn't hurt, but his car was ruined, and the carnage continued for the next several laps. Sterling Marlin wrecked twice. The first was a solo, as Marlin missed both walls and the cars around him slowed down quickly. But a few laps later he lost it again, slamming Dale Jarrett into the wall. The sparks were flying in front of Kyle and when he hit the brakes Morgan Shepherd rammed him from the rear. The blow sent him spinning into traffic and he hit Sterling Marlin who was bouncing off the wall.

Amazingly enough, Petty's car still ran and while the race was under caution and the cleanup crews were pulling debris from the track, he rushed it into the pits for repairs. There was a lot to be done—four shredded tires that had to be changed, twisted sheet metal to be pulled away. Most of the damage had occurred in the back. The spoiler was banged up, along with the opening that led to the gas tank. Still, there was nothing that couldn't be fixed. The trick was to do it without losing laps.

Robin was gambling that it would be a long caution. There was sheet metal scattered all over the track, which meant a lot of work for the cleanup crews. Robin decided they could pit several times— do a little work and rush back out before the lead car passed; then in again on the next time around. It was a nerve-wracking process that took three stops, but they got the tires changed and most of the sheet metal pulled away, and amazingly enough they didn't lose a lap.

When the race restarted, the car was flying. Petty passed Michael Waltrip, the King, Jim Sauter—some of the same people he had passed before the wreck. It was frustrating work on a crowded track, where only the lowest groove was fast, but Petty was battling and the crew was impressed. "You're faster than the leader," reported John Wilson.

They continued to work on the car during cautions, pulling away bent metal and adjusting the chassis, and somewhere after a hundred laps Robin pronounced the operation a success. "You've got the car now," he said, which was an encouraging thought since they were already the fastest thing on the track. They were proving once again that speed in qualifying was not the same thing as speed in the race. With thirty two competitors on a half-mile track, the key was to manage the car in traffic, and as the laps rolled by, Petty was a master. He made the top 10 at the halfway point and cracked the top 5 around lap 290. It was hard to stay there pitting on the back, but that was where he was running on lap 340 when there was another wreck on the track just ahead. Alan Kulwicki and Mark Martin were battling for third when they ran together and both of them spun. Martin was high and sliding toward Kulwicki, with Petty right behind and no place to go. Kyle knew he couldn't stop without being hit again from the rear. He stood on the gas and aimed for the opening between the spinning cars, which was closing in a hurry, the whole thing happening in a slow-motion blur. He made it through with only a bump.

The damage was minor, and as the race wound down he was in 4th place trying to catch Ken Schrader, who was 3rd. The computer said they would run out of gas, maybe with about two laps to go. Robin had to choose. Should they stop for gas, giving up hope of a top 5 finish, but assuring themselves of at least a top 10? Or should they go for broke? Robin didn't seem to agonize much. "We're gonna run to the end," he said.

They made it on fumes, finishing 4th in a race where they started 26th and had to battle their way through the wrecks. "That's a great job by everybody," said Felix.

"Kyle," he added, "you drove your ass off."

They came to Darlington on Labor Day weekend still sixth in the championship competition, but gaining in a hurry. They were only thirteen points out of 5th, sixty out of 4th, really within striking distance of 3rd—and the racing world was beginning to take notice. Publications like *Winston Cup Scene*, the tabloid bible of NASCAR racing, were ticking off Petty's stats since May: nine top 10s in the last twelve races, four top 5s and of course the win at Watkins Glen.

The story at Darlington was still Davey Allison. It was hard to imagine a season more dramatic—his wrecks, his brother, the championship race he had led for so long. And now, he was racing for a million dollars. The Southern 500 on Labor Day weekend was the last of the Big Four races in the sport. If Daytona was Mecca, and Talladega was the fastest track in NASCAR, and Charlotte was arguably the state of the art, Darlington was easily the most historic. It dated all the way to 1950, just about the time of the founding of NASCAR. A man by the name of Harold Brasington, a construction contractor in the Darlington area, had been to see the Indianapolis 500, and he came back home with a radical idea. Why couldn't stock cars race like that—on a speedway a mile or two in length, nicely paved with banking in the turns and speeds of more than one hundred mph? Why couldn't they have a Southern 500 and hold it every year right there in Darlington? Some people thought he had lost his mind. Stock cars raced on red clay tracks, and the tracks were short, and nobody raced for five hundred miles. The cars weren't built for that kind of punishment. The damn things would probably fly apart.

Brasington was stubborn enough to try it. He put together a group of investors, and built the first stock car superspeedway—a mile and a quarter, completely paved, with a gleaming grandstand to accommodate the crowds. Twenty thousand people came to see the first race (won by a driver named Johnny Mantz), and the crowds kept growing year after year. For a raw and fledgling backwoods sport, the track at Darlington was a major breakthrough.

Mr. Brasington never got rich from his vision. Not long after the track was built, he sold his stock and moved on to other things. Then, forty-two years later, he was back—being inducted this time into the racing hall of fame. He smiled and waved and received polite applause from the fans, but he seemed a little lost in the shuffle of celebrities. Politicians were there by the boatload. They always were at the Labor Day race, but now in the middle of a presidential election, everybody agreed they were thicker than usual. Sen. Strom Thurmond was there, the aging Republican from South Carolina, and he ended his speech with words sure to please: "God bless Richard Petty." Bill Clinton was more controversial. "Ole Slick Willie," muttered one grizzled fan. "Tried marijuana, but didn't inhale." Scattered cheers greeted Clinton's introduction, followed immediately by a crescendo of boos and the voice of a woman screaming from the crowd: "Draft-dodger!"

For the Democrats, it was a tough day at the track.

The guys in the pits, meanwhile, were indifferent. It was the morning of the race, and the sideshows were irrelevant—particularly to a crew like Davey Allison's, which was feeling the pressure of the past few weeks. First the tragedies, and now the possibility of a million dollar win. That was the bounty put up by Winston for any driver winning three of the circuit's Big Four. Davey had won the

Daytona 500 and the Winston 500 in Talladega. He missed in Charlotte, though, which meant that it all came down to this race.

In a way, the pressure was a welcome relief, a diversion from the pain, which Davey had handled with uncommon class—remaining gracious to the media and fans. "It has been tough on our family," he told Tom Higgins of the *Charlotte Observer.* "But the only thing different is that we're in the public eye. Tragic deaths like Clifford's happen to families all over the world, and they hurt just as much as we are."

Higgins was impressed with Allison's spirit—and yet you had to wonder what was happening inside, beneath that mantel of bravery and grace. Ryan Pemberton, Robin's younger brother, was a tire man for Davey, and he reported the whole team was feeling the strain. Robin guessed that it would probably get worse, for the team hadn't had a proper chance to grieve, but he didn't have time to think about it much—certainly not at the track, where he had his own worries as they waited for the race.

So far, the weekend had been a disaster. Petty's car was terrible on the first day of practice. The motor was sputtering, and they had to put in a new set of plugs, and when they finally got it running, the gears were wrong. "We've got a mess," said Jim Long mildly. They tinkered with it off and on all morning, and when they qualified on Friday afternoon, their time was appalling. They came in 30th out of thirty-eight cars. They planned to try it again on Saturday, but the monsoons fell on the Darlington track and second-round qualifying was cancelled.

There was only one consolation: The car was handling pretty well in the corners, and they thought with the last round of changes on Friday, the setup might be right for the race. They couldn't be sure. The rains on Saturday had washed out time they were counting on for practice. But on Sunday morning they were hoping for the best. This was no time to have a bad race.

The weather was moody on Sunday afternoon—muggy and warm, with rain clouds beginning to gather near the track. Kyle had to hope the showers stayed away. It would take some time to move up from 30th, and he didn't want to see the race cut short.

As always, he started fast—passing Musgrave, Marcis and Mast, and hoping for the best. It was a little disconcerting to be near the back. This was the place where the wrecks usually happened, particularly in the early stages of the race, when drivers like himself were impatient to pass, and the ones they were passing were seldom as good.

Today, however, the Lady in Black was with him—this mysterious track that seemed to have a mind and spirit of its own. There was probably no place on the NASCAR circuit that commanded greater awe. Turn 4 was the toughest, with cars coming out of it inches from the wall. One mistake, and your race day was over. But Petty's Pontiac was handling well, and after thirty-one laps he had moved all the way to 15th place. He was faster than the leader, Sterling Marlin, when the caution came out on lap 37. All the cars came in for new tires, and the Petty crew knew they had to be good. They were pitting on the backstretch, as they had in Bristol, and once again it was a major disadvantage. Their front-stretch rivals were back on the track by the time Kyle's car was up on the jacks. To make matters worse, a lug nut fell from the left front tire, and they lost precious seconds as Robin retrieved it. "Sorry," he grumbled, but Petty's reply on the radio was breezy.

"That's okay, man, we'll get 'em."

They were in 22nd place when the race restarted, but thirty laps later they were back to 14th and bearing down on Alan Kulwicki. They had passed good cars in rapid succession—Bill Elliott, Darrell Waltrip, Derrike Cope—but Petty was beginning to notice a problem. The car was pushing going in to turn 1, the left front sliding as it might in snow, and for the first time all day he had to back off. Elliott passed him on lap 89, something nobody else had done, and Petty was grateful when it came time to pit.

The stop this time went smoothly enough, and after the first few laps under green, the Mello Yello car once again was flying. Petty was ninth at the halfway point, and still gaining ground, when he glanced at the temperature dials on the dash. The oil was fine, but the water was getting high, and it brought back memories of the race in the spring. It had been a disaster: Their engine was hot and blew because of too much tape and debris on the grill. That was the maddening thing about the sport. There were a million variables you had to control, a million disasters to be headed off— and if you did it just right, and luck was with you, that merely put you in *position* to win. Even then, there were no guarantees. All you could do was hang in there and try hard not to repeat your mistakes.

This time they caught the problem soon enough; the temperature was still at 195, and Robin was sure it would be all right. He was actually more worried about the weather. In the infield behind him, the Confederate flags were snapping in the wind, and by lap 250 the gusts were swirling and whipping up dust and the clouds were turning the color of a bruise.

Out on the track, they were in good shape. Petty was passing Ken Schrader to move up to 8th, and he made it to 7th as they pitted for tires. But Steve Knipe's voice brought ominous news. "Stay with it," he said. "There's a little bit of rain in turn one."

Ten laps later, it was raining hard. The caution flag came out, and after a few more minutes they stopped the race, waiting to see if the rain would pass.

It didn't look good, and the only person happy was Darrell Waltrip. When the best cars pitted, he stayed on the track, which meant he was now the leader of the race. His best chance for victory lay with the rain, and every now and then he would do a little dance, trying to coax more moisture from the skies.

Some people found his act too precious, but in a way it was easy enough to understand. In the course of Waltrip's outstanding career (eighty-three wins going into Darlington, which put him 4th all-time, one win behind the great Bobby Allison), he had never yet won the Southern 500. This time, with the help of the rains, he did. With a mist still falling at 6 P.M., NASCAR decided to call the race.

Davey Allison took it with a smile, despite a million dollars down the drain. His car had run well (in fact had led a good part of the day), and the weather was something nobody could control. A few trucks away, Kyle Petty felt the same. He had had a good run from 30th to 7th. There was nothing to do now but grin and move on.

"Next week," he said, "there's always another one."

CHAPTER 11

BATTLING BACK

They came to Richmond with a dull sense of dread. Kyle had gotten his first win in the city, but that was on the old Richmond track. He had never done very well at the new one, which was nestled in a corner of the state fairgrounds—and in fact their performance at the race in March was one of the worst they had had all year. They finished 20th and were lucky to get that. They thought they had learned a few things from it, or at least they hoped, for the pressure was mounting to do well every race.

They were still 6th in the points, still hoping for more. "Mathematically," said Robin, "we could make it to 3rd. Optimistically, to 4th. Realistically, to 5th." To move up at all, they would have to be fast in the last eight races.

They brought a new car to Richmond this time—a sleek Grand Prix they had named James Dean. Actually, they had run it the year before, but crashed it so badly at a race in Bristol that it had to be completely rebuilt—a new rear end and a new nose like the one they had made for Watkins Glen. Robin thought the nose was a breakthrough, a major improvement in their aerodynamics, which had been the Pontiacs' problem all year. Now the whole picture was beginning to brighten. The aerodynamics were slowly getting better, and the competitors were entering a stretch of the season where the tracks were shorter, and horsepower and handling were now more important. Those were areas a team could control. They could build good motors and find a chassis setup that worked, and in Robin's mind there was no reason now why they shouldn't excel.

He knew, however, that Richmond was tricky. It was three quarters of a mile, with a shape that resembled a lopsided "D." The backstretch was straight, but the front was not, which meant you were turning most of the time. It was hard on the tires, and as Jim Long said, the setup had to be "right on the money." The worst part was, the September race was always at night, when the track was cool, while the practice sessions were in the daytime. If the car was perfect in the middle of the day, the chances were good that the setup would be a little off for the race. All you could do, said Robin, was get the car close in the late afternoon, then play your best hunch on the final adjustments.

He felt pretty good about the way it was going. Though they had qualified 17th—unimpressive once again—the car was much better than that in practice, maybe top 5. There were a lot of others, however, that were right in there—Ernie Irvan, Ricky Rudd, Rusty Wallace. Rusty, in fact, seemed as strong as he had been all year. So did Earnhardt. Geoff Bodine and Ken Schrader looked good. Allison and Kulwicki were always quick. If they all guessed right on their final adjustments, it ought to be a race. Robin wasn't worried about the other cars, though. He was nervous, instead, about his own.

"It looks pretty good in the corners," he said. "But I don't know. It might be too perfect."

Robin smiled when he said it. He knew he had invented a new way to worry.

* * *

When the race began, Dick Seidenspinner headed down to turn 4. Seidenspinner is the business manager for the Kyle Petty team. At thirty-three, he's a handsome guy who resembles Tom Cruise, with a personality more like Peter Pan. "This is the place," he said, and he climbed on the back of a flatbed truck that was parked maybe twenty yards from the track. There was a chain-link fence for protection in between, but he was close enough to feel the fury—the roar of the engines and the squeal of the tires—to see the rotors turning red in the brakes. "Is this a great sport or what?" He grinned.

For Petty, the first few miles were hard. He was trapped in the middle in a large group of cars, and it took him nearly thirty laps to break free. Finally, however, he got around Trickle and Geoff Bodine and slashed between Hensley and Morgan Shepherd. He caught Terry Labonte a few laps later, passed him low going into turn 1, and all of a sudden he was moving up in a hurry. "Good job, Kyle," said John Wilson softly.

Rusty Wallace, by now, was leading the race, and his car—a Pontiac like Kyle's—was handling so well he was already beginning to lap the slower traffic. Kyle, however, was just as fast, passing Dale Jarrett and Kenny Schrader to move up to tenth. By lap 85, he had made the top 5, and his lap times now were the fastest on the track.

Watching from the turn, Seidenspinner was impressed. "This," he said, "is the best we've ever run at this place."

Disaster in racing can happen in a hurry, however. This time, it came on the first pit stop. Kyle and several others came in to change tires, and just as they were ready to return to the track, Jim Sauter lost control in the turn. His car went spinning and brought out the caution, which meant that Petty was down one lap. Steve Knipe urged him to stand on the gas and beat the leader, Ernie Irvan, to the flag.

Petty's reply on the radio was angry. "I can't do shit," he said. "I got a flat tire."

That was the second ingredient of disaster.

As Petty was starting to leave the pit, he had pulled in front of Dick Trickle, who was just coming in. Trickle rammed him and flattened his tire, and Petty had to limp around the track. Irvan passed him before he got to the flag, which meant that Petty was now two laps down. It was incredible, really. Here he was, a top-5 car and still moving up when the mistakes of other drivers put him deep in the hole.

In the confusion of the moment, Petty wasn't sure how bad it was, and Robin didn't have the heart to tell him. "You're the last car on the lead lap," he said. He later explained that he didn't think Petty was "in the mood" to hear the truth. More than that, Robin didn't want to dishearten his driver with three hundred laps still to go in the race—but even before it was over, he came to regard his deception as silly. Kyle Petty, he decided, was not a driver who needed to be coddled.

Actually, Robin had known that before, but the race in Richmond was a moment of truth, when he could feel his respect jump a notch on the graph. Not just for Kyle, but for the whole team, really. This was a night when nobody quit.

Petty was 24th when the race restarted, but his lap times were fast. He passed Ken Schrader and Brett Bodine, and after a few more laps when he got his rhythm, he passed the 2nd-place car of Ernie Irvan. "You're driving your ass off," said Robin. "Man, I appreciate it." Slowly in the pit, the expressions were changing—from downcast eyes to smiles of satisfaction, and when Petty came in on lap 230, they changed four tires in nineteen seconds. "Great stop, guys," said Felix Sabates, and now you could feel it beginning to build. Two laps was a lot to make up without help, but it was clear that the guys were giving it a shot.

Back on the track, Kyle battled past Kulwicki. It took two laps running side by side, as Kulwicki veered and tried to drive Petty to the apron of the track. "What a dickhead he is," muttered Kyle, but then he was past and his sights were set on the leaders of the race. At that moment, there was a two-way battle for first—Darrell Waltrip and Rusty Wallace, side by side and six inches apart, careening through the turns. Wallace was running on the high side of the track, with Waltrip just below him, and the battle went on for more than twenty laps. Through the whole thing, Kyle was gaining. He drove past Waltrip and pulled even with Wallace on lap 280. He tried to pass, but couldn't make it and had to drop back. Two laps later, he tried again, diving low on the track, and now their cars were side by side—a repeat of Wallace's battle with Waltrip. But Petty was faster than either of them, and after two laps he was pulling away.

"We've passed every single car on the race track today," said Felix.

"Yeah," agreed Robin, "and still a lap down."

"It's ain't over yet," said Felix.

Essentially it was. Wallace was too strong for Petty to catch him again. All Kyle could do as the race wound down was try to gain as many spots as he could. He was 17th with fifty laps to go, but he soon passed his father and Jimmy Hensley, and then Dale Jarrett to move to 14th. He was now chasing Elliott and Terry Labonte, and both of them had a good lead on him. Elliott was 3.5 seconds ahead with twenty-eight laps to go in the race—but Petty was gaining a half second each lap, and it didn't take long to get around him.

With ten laps to go, he was catching Labonte, but the traffic was thick as he pulled out to pass, and Brett Bodine clipped him from the rear. Petty nearly spun and when he regained control Labonte had pulled to a six-length lead. "You've got seven laps to get back to him," said Robin.

Petty didn't answer, but he was chipping away. With six laps to go, he was four lengths back; with three to go, he was on Labonte's bumper—and the next time around the track, he passed him.

"Great job," said Robin. "Just bring it back."

Rusty Wallace won the race—a good day for Pontiacs. Petty was 12th, which dropped him to 7th in the championship standings, but Felix Sabates felt good about it.

"Kyle," he said, "the whole world knew you were here."

Petty was silent, too frustrated at the moment to talk. But he admitted to a reporter a few minutes later that he had a good feeling about the weeks just ahead.

It was mid-September, and they were in the middle of a difficult stretch—eight straight races without a break. The next stop was Dover, and Kyle headed north on his motorcycle. It was a pretty ride from North Carolina, eight hours through the hills of Virginia, across the Chesapeake to the Eastern Shore, and then through the plains of western Delaware. Time to think, to be by himself. He didn't have those moments very often.

These days he was thinking a lot about his team. There were times in the past when he had seen as much talent—certainly at the Wood Brothers' when he won his first races. But there was something special about the chemistry this time, something that Robin brought to the team. It was amazing, really. Robin had come over from Mark Martin's crew and brought no one with him, accepting instead the people who were here. Slowly but surely he had won their trust. There had been some moments of friction and doubt— a few clashes, for example, with Richard Bostic, the team's truck driver. In general, though, Robin as a leader was honest and fair, and eager for the people around him to shine. Back in Richmond, Kyle had told one reporter about the changes he had seen in the demeanor of John Wilson. "I didn't know John *had* a personality," he said. But now John smiled and his eyes were wry and full of amusement, and he no longer lived on stomach antacids. Kyle gave Robin the credit for that.

It wasn't just Robin. Jim Sutton, Jim Long, Barry Cook, Steve Knipe . . . they had a pretty good supporting cast, and Kyle could see good things in the future, maybe a championship down the line. When he got to Dover, a reporter asked him how he felt about that, and whether he ever worried about the downside of fame. Petty had just returned from a dinner at Sambo's, a little neon diner down near the coast, where the race teams gathered for boiled shrimp and beer. A lot of guys headed from there to the bars and a few more hours of Friday night carousing. Petty did not. There was a time when he partied as hard as the rest, drinking, chasing women, whatever was on the agenda for the night. It was the fast-lane life of a kid in racing, but he was older now, with serious goals, and he also had an image to protect. His father had taught him a few things about that, how an image will betray you if it's false or contrived, but not if it's part of who you are. The trick was to balance the public and the private, and Richard Petty was a master at that. He had refused to lose that connection with himself, or his small-town raising in Level Cross. Kyle was grateful to have that model. He never expected to replace Richard Petty, but the fans and the media were hungry for stars, and Kyle was hungry for a championship season.

"If it happens, it happens," he said with a grin. "A big part of fame is how you think about it. I'll still know I'm full of shit."

Despite their improvement since the first race of the season, which had given the team such hope for the future, their performance since Watkins Glen had been strange. They had raced well enough, with determined charges to the front of the pack, but their practice sessions were always a struggle, and their qualifying times were mediocre at best. That pattern continued again in Dover. In practice Friday, they were nearly a half second off the pace, and on Friday afternoon they qualified 16th. Partly it was a reflection of Robin's priorities. He was less concerned with qualifying setups—those combinations of gears and springs, tire pressure and shocks that would make the car go fast for a lap. Instead, he was interested in race setups, which needed to last for five hundred miles. The team hit it right most of the time, and when race day came, the car was strong. Still, there were dangers in starting from the middle or the back—an added strain on the driver and the car, and a much greater chance of being in a wreck. "We need to qualify better," said Petty, but there was no use worrying about it now. Their concern at the moment was Sunday afternoon.

As usual, there were headaches—a rain that interrupted their practice on Saturday, and then a problem with the engine Sunday morning. Barry Cook, one of John Wilson's most capable assistants, was poking around underneath the hood when he discovered that the rocker arms were old. Those were metal parts that made the engine valves open and close, and in a race this long they had to be new. Robin hated to do it just hours before the race, but there was really no choice. They had to tear the engine apart, and put in new arms. "I'm tired of rebuilding shit," he growled, but at least they caught the problem in time, and when the green flag fell Robin thought they were ready.

For the first hundred laps, the verdict was encouraging. Petty started in a cluster of good cars, with Sterling Marlin beside him and Bill Elliott and Darrell Waltrip just ahead. He had moved up a spot by lap 13, when Kenny Schrader hit the wall. "What do you want?" asked Robin, as they got ready to pit. "All four tires?"

"You make the call," said Petty. "I just ride around." He was feeling loose and confident right now. On a crowded track, his car was fast, and when the race restarted he moved up to 10th. Thirty laps later, another caution and a dazzling nineteen-second pit stop put him in 7th, and there was a round of smiles and high fives in the pit. Things were still going well on lap 89. Petty was chasing Alan Kulwicki, who was side by side in the turns with Chad Little. All of a sudden, there was a cloud of smoke. Little and Kulwicki had run together, and Kulwicki was sliding hard towards the wall. In the bank of smoke produced by the tires, it was impossible for Petty to see where to go. "Stand on it!" yelled Steve Knipe, who could see the whole track from the spotter's tower. Petty did, and he made it past as Kulwicki hit the wall and bounced back toward him.

A few minutes later, he had another scare coming out of the pits, when he and Morgan Shepherd ran together—but there was no real harm to either car. "It was gentle," said Robin.

Back on the track, new tires and a chassis adjustment seemed to help, and Petty once again was moving up. He made it to 4th on lap 180, when his voice came on the radio again. "Out of gas, man," he said. It was the first ingredient in a moment of disaster that looked like Richmond all over again. His engine sputtered and quit altogether, and he coasted around the one-mile track, losing precious time. When he made it to the pit and the car was finally ready to go, he couldn't get it started. The crew pushed him off and the engine caught, but then a caution flag came out. He was nearly two laps down by now, when NASCAR hit him with the final indignity. The officials penalized him for speeding. They said he was fast coming into pit road, and in a way it was hard for Petty to argue. Race cars aren't equipped with speedometers. The drivers use tacometers to gauge pit speeds, and when the engine quit, so, of course, did Petty's tacometer. He tried to estimate by staying even with Derrike Cope, who happened to be pitting at exactly the same time. Since Cope wasn't penalized, Petty assumed his speed was okay. Robin tried to explain the situation to a NASCAR official standing near his pit. "Be reasonable," he pleaded, but the official walked away.

"The official from hell," Robin muttered to the crew.

When the race restarted, Petty was listed as one lap down with the leader, Bill Elliott, right behind him. If Elliott got by, they were in deep trouble—two laps down with the race coming up to the halfway point. Petty's car had developed a push, the front tires sliding just a little in the turns, but for sixty laps he held Elliott off, and finally a caution flag came out. Petty was 12th in the race by now—3rd among cars that were one lap down—and this was the moment when everything changed. On the restart, Dale Earnhardt, who was just ahead of Petty, clipped the bumper of the 10th-place car of Geoff Bodine and sent him spinning. As the caution came out, Earnhardt passed the leader, Ernie Irvan, who had moved ahead of Elliott. Earnhardt was back on the lead lap again, and with Bodine in a wreck and out of the way, Petty was now first among the cars a lap down.

As always, when the race restarted, the lapped cars were on the inside groove, the leaders outside, which put Petty and Irvan side by side. They hit the first turn and Petty pulled ahead, and he was up by a length at the end of one lap. Four laps later, his lead was growing when Jim Sauter hit the wall coming out of turn 2. The caution came out, and there were cheers in the pit. With the help of this string of well-timed wrecks, Petty had battled from nearly two laps down, and was now, once again, in the thick of the race.

The drama, however, was not yet over. The track was slicker than it had been all day, with the rubber of nearly three hundred laps, and there was another big crash when the race restarted—ten cars this time, triggered by the spin of Dick Trickle's Ford. Trickle bounced off the wall and began a helpless slide down the bank, squarely into the path of the oncoming traffic. Derrike Cope and Kyle dove low to avoid him, while others began to crash all around. Petty, again, made it through by a whisker.

"I think we've used up our luck," said Knipe.

Petty laughed. "Ten-four on that."

Fortunately, the need for luck had passed. When they finally got started without a wreck, the race moved quickly and cleanly to the end. Petty was 7th and moving up, and the crew chipped in an amazing pit stop—a four-tire change in less than nineteen seconds.

They finished third, and Petty, as usual, gave credit to the team. "You guys were great," he said, as soon as he crossed the finish line. "Thank you."

Such testimonials are common among the drivers, even those with colder personalities. Alan Kulwicki, for example, was one of the coldest—notorious around the NASCAR garage for driving his team to the breaking point. In Dover, however, he let them know he was grateful. Kulwicki had wrecked and finished 34th, which was a blow to his hopes for a championship. He had been in 3rd place when the race began, within easy striking distance of the top. Now he knew it was a much harder road, and he could have sulked about his own misfortune. Instead, he called the team together and told them he appreciated what they had done. "This probably takes us out of the point race," he said, "but I just want to say I'm proud of you and what we've done anyway."

As the *Charlotte Observer*'s Tom Higgins noted, it was "a touching scene—" but Kulwicki's sentiment was premature, for the championship race was not yet over. In fact, it was getting steadily tighter, with six or seven drivers in the range of the top. Everybody knew, when they thought about it, that there was a lot of hard racing still to come.

The next stop on the tour was Martinsville, which, back in April, had been the low point of Kyle Petty's year. There had been dissension between the team and Felix Sabates, and the race had ended in a frightening wreck—Petty's car bursting into flames underneath him. Robin didn't tell many people at the time, but he had been so discouraged on that particular Sunday that he had thought of going back to the restaurant business—his family's profession in upstate New York. The year before, when he was Mark Martin's crew chief, he had grown tired of the tantrums of the owner, Jack Roush. For awhile in the spring, he wasn't really sure that Felix was different and life was too short for the aggravation; but now he was beginning to change his mind. Sabates did have a temper, and it was never very pleasant when he let it fly; but the explosions came and went in a hurry, and in between Sabates was full of fun. He shouldered the team's ups and downs as his own, and when things went badly, as they had a couple of weeks earlier in Richmond, he was quick to push his own feelings aside. "I'm proud of you," he told the guys. But he was at his best when things went well, lavish in his showers of praise and rewards. Rolex watches were his favorite. He seemed to take delight in the sheer extravagance, and he understood that his gestures were good for morale.

Robin could work for a guy like that, and he was beginning to think, as they came back to Martinsville, that this was a week they would make Felix proud. Their first few hours of practice were spectacular. They were easily the fastest car on the track, and though a few others were slowly catching up, they thought they had a good shot at the pole. Certainly they had worked at it harder this time with a qualifying setup that was a little more risky. They had put a heavy spring on the right rear wheel, which made the car much looser in the turns, and as practice ended on Friday afternoon, only Geoff Bodine was as fast.

Qualifying began under threatening clouds, and Petty was praying that the rain would stay away. He was ready now—antsy, in fact, as the drivers began to run their laps. Some of the early times were good. Jimmy Hensley's best lap was 20.6 seconds, about what Kyle was running in practice, but one by one, the others fell short: Alan Kulwicki ran a 20.8, Ernie Irvan a 20.7. Then came Petty, the 17th car to take the track, and his time was easily the fastest of the day: 20.4, just over 92 mph. He smiled a little as he climbed from the car, but he knew he couldn't afford to celebrate. There were sixteen drivers still to go, and included in the group was Geoff Bodine.

Bodine, however, didn't have a good lap. He was four tenths slower than he had been in practice, and Petty won his second pole of the year. Now his smile was unrestrained. "How was that?" he asked one reporter, and he began to reminisce about the Martinsville track. It had been pretty kind to the Petty family. His father had won fifteen races there, and Kyle remembered the late afternoons, playing with the other racetrack kids—the Pearsons, the Allisons and whoever was around.

"We had a game," he said. "There was an old manual scoreboard then. Two men posted the numbers of the top 5 cars by hand. Me and my sisters would rush to that scoreboard when the races were over and put Daddy's number in all five spots. Then the Pearson boys would come over and cover the scoreboard with David's number, 17, and then here would come the Allison bunch, and they would take the 17s down and replace 'em with 12s. Back then, the track was covered with so much rubber that we would make balls out of it to throw at each other and try to keep the rival bunch away. When my family left Martinsville, 43 was usually up there. Daddy always stayed until the last fan that wanted one had gotten an autograph. We were the last people to leave the track."

Petty laughed and shook his head. "I can't think of a better place to win."

Race day came with soggy skies—low, gray clouds and a fine mist falling, as a fleet of wreckers tried to dry the track. They ran lap after lap, pulling old tires that were hooked to a chain, but the mist was slowly turning to rain and the wreckers finally quit. It was dismal now, the water standing in pools on the track, and NASCAR decided to call it a day. It was the first rainout of the '92 season, and there was nothing to do but come back tomorrow.

They did come back to more rain clouds, but the mist let up around the middle of the day, and just before 2:30 they were off. Kyle was shaky for the first few laps. He was driving James Dean, their Richmond car, and it felt a little loose. Partly, it was the difference in the Martinsville track. In Richmond, you were turning all the time, while this was two dragstrips with hard, flat turns at either end. The straightaways required a powerful motor, but as Petty explained to ESPN, "You've got to get through the turns to use it."

Starting from the pole, he led the first laps, but Hensley and Ernie Irvan were both pushing hard, and Hensley took the lead after only five laps. "Your tires are cold," said Robin. "They'll come in." Five laps later they were beginning to stick, and Kyle passed Hensley coming out of turn 4. The car was starting to feel pretty good, but Ernie Irvan got around Hensley too, and he and Kyle were still in a battle. On the 30th lap, they were side by side, but Kyle held him off, and ten laps later he was stretching his lead. By lap 52, he was six lengths ahead and pulling away so quickly that Robin began to wonder if he was pushing too hard. "Take care of your brakes," he said, his voice a little anxious, as Petty roared past him into turn 1. There was no reply, but the laps ticked away and the car was fine. Petty had a two-second lead over Irvan, then two and a half, and by lap 100, with Rusty Wallace now in 2nd place, Kyle had stretched the lead to a full five seconds.

It was up to eight by lap 140 when they hit their first trouble spot of the day. Once again, they ran out of gas. Déjà vu. Petty coasted to the pit, and when the car was gassed it wouldn't crank. Robin couldn't believe it was happening again. He thought it said something about their maturity. As a team, they were making too many mistakes, but they did their best to recover, pushing the car until the engine finally caught and Petty went roaring back to the track. Fortunately, the leaders were beginning to pit, with scheduled stops for gas and tires, and Robin did his best to reassure Kyle. "I'm sorry about the gas, but we're okay. You are *not* a lap down."

Out on the track, Petty was still fast and making up ground, and when Bill Elliott hit the wall on lap 160, it gave everybody a chance to pit. After a good stop, Kyle was 3rd when the race restarted. He got off quickly, and pulled outside of Geoff Bodine when disaster hit again. Bodine was loose coming out of the turns, and with Kyle beside him, he began to slide up the concrete banking. The collision sent Petty spinning into traffic. "Son of a bitch!" yelled Robin, as Petty came to rest in the middle of the track, his rear end pointed in the wrong direction and cars swerving madly to avoid a collision. The frustration by now was nearly overwhelming—such good cars in the last few weeks, and so many holes to dig out of. But Steve Knipe's voice put things in perspective: "We still have 325 laps to go." When they thought about it that way, it wasn't so bad. Even after the wreck and running out of gas, they were only one lap down in the race; the car was fast and there was plenty of time. "We'll get 'em," said Robin. "Just hang in there."

For the next sixty laps, Petty battled through traffic, passing Davey, Dale Jarrett, and Morgan Shepherd, and by lap 240 he had a clear shot at the leader, Rusty Wallace. The crowd was cheering for him now. He was three lengths back and bearing down, and every time he got close to Rusty's bumper, a roar of approval swept through the stands. Petty was ninth and still a lap down, but if he got by Rusty, he was back in the race. Wallace, however, was having none of it. His Pontiac was strong on the straightaways, while Kyle was clearly more efficient in the turns. Yet lap after lap, Rusty cut down to block him, and the people in the stands were now on their feet. On lap 300, Kyle was one length back, and five laps later he was on Rusty's bumper when they caught the slower car of the King. Kyle dove low as Richard Petty drifted high, and Rusty was left with nowhere to go. After a one-on-one of nearly fifty miles, he was back on the lead lap and hungry for more. "Good job, Kyle," said John Wilson.

A few laps later, they got a caution flag, and Kyle was seventh after pitting for tires. Unfortunately, their problems for the day were not yet over. Kyle had made it all the way to fourth, and his car was as fast as any on the track, when there was a collision just ahead on lap 370. Petty hit the brakes, but Dick Trickle couldn't stop and rammed him from behind, and Petty went sliding into the grass. His tires became firmly stuck in the mud, spinning wildly every time he hit the gas, but the car wouldn't move. "Just send a wrecker," he said, and his voice was angry. But the mud was so bad the wrecker got stuck, and Kyle by now was two laps down, yelling frantically for someone to push him. Richard Bostic and a couple of guys on the crew went running toward the grass, joined by Danny Myers, a longtime buddy from Earnhardt's team, whose driver was already out of the race. Together, they managed to push him off, but he was two laps down with just over one hundred laps to go, and the chances were slim that he would have a good finish.

Petty, however, was too mad to quit. His car was still fast, and when they caught a caution on lap 389 he was first among the cars that were two laps down. Almost immediately after the restart, he passed the leader, Geoff Bodine, which meant that he was now only one lap down. "Kyle has put on a show here today," declared Ned Jarrett of ESPN, and the show wasn't over. Petty was battling through traffic again, and after fifty laps and another caution, he had another clear shot at the leader. On lap 442, he passed him, and the people in the stands were screaming again. Amazingly, he had battled from two laps down, and there were fifty-eight laps to go in the race.

Petty didn't win, but he kept moving up and came in fourth. He climbed from the car looking satisfied and tired, and told a crowd of reporters: "I can't say enough about the crew."

The crew, however, was buying none of that. "How about the driver?" said Robin. He didn't try to hide the admiration in his voice.

On his way back to Charlotte, Richard Bostic's radio was crackling. He was always proud to drive the Mello Yello truck, with its bright, flashing colors and Kyle Petty logo, but never more so than after this race. Fifteen or twenty times on the three-hour drive, other truckers hailed him on the CB: "Hell of a race, Mello Yello." Richard beamed every time he heard it, and he shared the feeling of the other guys on the team that there was nothing now that they couldn't accomplish. Their driver clearly was one of the best, and the team itself was slowly getting there. They had their glitches—running out of gas in two straight races—but there were also the 18-second pit stops, which were becoming the envy of the NASCAR world.

Robin, too, felt the surge in morale, and his instincts told him it was more than superficial. If he had any doubts, they were erased. Tuesday morning when he arrived at the shop just after eight o'clock. He had been thinking on the way about all they would have to do to the car, which had been so badly battered in the wrecks. But when he walked in the door, the crew was already hard at work, and half the repairs were already done. Robin smiled. "These guys," he said, "are getting pretty hungry."

CHAPTER 12

RETURN TO VICTORY LANE

More rain was waiting in North Wilkesboro. They got the qualifying in okay, and Kyle was strong, finishing fourth. But then the monsoons hit on the morning of the race, and there was nothing to do but try to wait it out. The guys on the crew were watching X-rated movies, and Robin and Kyle and a few other people were sitting in the truck telling rain-delay stories. The tallest tale, allegedly true, came from Tom Higgins of the *Charlotte Observer*. Higgins is a veteran reporter and fan who is such a fixture on the NASCAR circuit that he has his own racing card like the drivers. He said there was a Sunday in North Wilkesboro, back sometime in the 1960s, when it rained so hard that the worms began crawling from the waterlogged ground, and millions of them slithered to the track and died. The rain finally stopped, but the track was so coated and slimey by now that it was impossible to race. Higgins said that as far as he knew, it was the only race ever called because of worms.

This time, they remained in the ground, however, but the rain was steady and showed no signs of going away. "I don't like these days," said Robin. "It's hard to get your adrenaline just right." All they could do was fidget, while the rains got worse as the day went along. Finally, the race was postponed until Monday, and even then a steady mist was falling. But they could see a break in the clouds to the south, a hint of blue sky out there in the distance, and they were able to race in the early afternoon. Kyle started fast. He moved up quickly from 4th to 3rd, and after ten laps he was challenging Rusty Wallace for 2nd. After twenty-five laps, they both passed the leader, Alan Kulwicki, and three laps later Kyle passed Rusty and took over the lead. Down in the pit, Bob Romano and the others were clapping. It had the feel of Martinsville again, with Kyle in a car that seemed to be dominant—and so far at least, there had been no disasters.

Then, about lap 50, they began to worry. Kyle was picking his way through the traffic, weaving between Derrike Cope and Wally Dallenbach, when Geoff Bodine started cutting the lead. He had passed Rusty Wallace to take over 2nd, and now he was setting his sights on Kyle. By lap 67, they were side by side, and two laps later Bodine made it past. Petty reported that the car was loose, but it was hard to hear exactly what he said. Something was wrong with the radio signal, and their voices were battling with a wave of static. Robin was furious. They needed to be able to discuss these things, talk about exactly what adjustments to make. Still, they knew they needed to tighten the chassis, and they did their best on the first pit stop.

After a while, the car was smoother, and so was the race. In fact, it was eerie out there on the track, as the laps rolled by without a wreck—without any kind of caution at all. This was North Wilkesboro, after all, which often resembled a demolition derby. Not today. The guys were racing hard and clean, and at the halfway point Kyle had settled into 3rd position. That was where he finished. Bodine and Mark Martin were both too fast, and Petty was fading badly at the end—losing ground to Rusty Wallace, who was two lengths behind him with two laps to go. Petty held on, and emerged from the car with a satisfied smile. These top 5s were getting to be a habit—and although he didn't want to talk about it much, he was beginning to feel the possibility of a win.

The next stop was Charlotte, with Rockingham after that, and his chances, he knew, were as good as anybody's. The hard part was trying to avoid the distractions, which came in many forms. For one thing, the farewell to his father was gaining momentum, and it was hard to avoid being caught up in it. Charlotte was the home of Humpy Wheeler, the P. T. Barnum of stock car racing, who knew a good thing when he saw it, and as president of the Charlotte Motor Speedway, was determined to promote it as hard as he could. The truth was, Wheeler revered Richard Petty. He saw him as a throwback to the athletes of old—to a football player like Otto Graham, or maybe a boxer like Muhammad Ali—men who were known for their toughness and fire, but who never built walls between themselves and the fans.

"All those guys left themselves totally open," said Wheeler. "That's why people love Richard Petty. In 1967, when he won twenty-seven races, I watched him at North Wilkesboro come back from seven laps down and win the race, and then spend three and a half hours signing autographs. Who would do that today? I'm not saying that the man is perfect; he's very opinionated, for one thing. I remember going to a race at the Caraway Speedway outside of Asheboro [North Carolina], where he was doing a promotional appearance. We got in his van and he was arguing with me about something we were doing that he didn't like, and fans would come up for autographs. He would roll down the window and smile, and after he had chatted and signed his name, he would roll it back up and give me hell. Richard never pitched his tantrums in public. He has such patience and self-control, an ability to smile. But the man is tough. He could take adversity and keep on going, and as an athlete he was willing to drive when he was hurt. His wreck in Daytona [in 1988, when Petty flipped five times and his car flew apart and the pieces were rammed by two other drivers] was the kind that mentally retires a lot of drivers. It would have been easy to say, 'That's it.' "

As far as Humpy Wheeler could tell, however, Petty was undaunted, and in a career that was littered with horrifying wrecks, he never missed a race unless his injuries were crippling. There was a day, for example, in 1986 when he crashed during a practice run in Charlotte. He hit the wall coming into turn three and knocked himself out—and the car began to burn as it rolled around the track. Kyle was one of the first ones to him, helping to pull his father from the car. When the King came to he said he was fine, just a little headache. He spent the night in a Charlotte hospital, but the next morning early he was back at the track, announcing that he planned to race on Sunday. He climbed gingerly into his backup car, and gripped the steering wheel in his hands. "*Unnnnnn . . . unnn . . . unnnn,*" he said with a grin, like a kid behind the wheel of his family's car. A reporter from Norfolk, Frank Vehorn, recorded the scene, and as far as Humpy Wheeler was concerned, it was one of those moments that defined Richard Petty—a reflection of his elemental joy in the sport.

Wheeler, of course, had seen the downside, too. Back in 1983, Petty had won a race at the Charlotte track, using illegal tires and an oversized engine—but it was a measure of Petty's standing in the sport that most people believed him when he said he didn't know. Whatever the truth, in Wheeler's mind it was one episode in a long career, and now in 1992, the time had finally come to say good-bye. Humpy intended to do it in style. He proclaimed the signing of Petty's millionth autograph (he was guessing, of course, but nobody cared), and gave prizes to the fans, and had forty-three skydivers jumping from a plane.

Even without Wheeler's showmanship, the media alone could have made it a circus. Correspondents were there from all over the world, lining up for interviews and scrambling for anecdotes and bits of information, and some of them began to spill over to Kyle. Many of their questions were trite and repetitious, but he did his best to be polite. He said it was an honor to talk about his father.

One of the questions that recurred was whether, when the season was finally over, there would be anyone to fill the void. Richard Petty had his own answer to it. He said he thought there would be no void, for there were too many other good drivers in the sport; but Kyle thought the issue was much more subtle. His father, he said, was a NASCAR legend, and legends did not come along over-night. They took shape slowly, over the space of decades, and it was impossible to be sure if any were emerging. Dale Earnhardt, maybe. Time would tell. But legends were not the same as stars, who were known to burst on the scene in a flash. Some, of course, were already established—Darrell Waltrip, Bill Elliott, Rusty Wallace—and there was a whole new wave of drivers in their thirties, all of them just now hitting their prime. Davey Allison was the most successful so far, but the group included Mark Martin and Kyle, as well as Ernie Irvan and Alan Kulwicki. All of those guys were capable of greatness, and it was almost certain that some would achieve it. But Petty grew nostalgic when he talked about stars, for the brightest of the group was no longer with them. Tim Richmond died in 1989, a victim of AIDS.

"He was a really, really good guy," said Kyle, "and a truly exceptional race car driver. He would have been the caliber of Dale Earnhardt or Richard Petty. People didn't accept him right off the bat. He was different. He had some class about him—he knew how to walk and talk, how to speak, which fork you were supposed to use at the table."

Richmond was thirty-four when he died, an Ohio native who was bright and flamboyant—in some ways a throwback to Curtis Turner and others from the 1960s, who knew how to party and have a good time. His image was much too flashy for the sport though. He let his hair grow long, and he always had pretty women at his side, and NASCAR didn't know quite what to do with him. But the man could drive. He won thirteen races in his short career, and there would have been more if he hadn't been sick. There was a whispering, of course, about what went wrong. Did he use drugs? Was he gay? Or was it heterosexual promiscuity? To Kyle, it didn't matter. Richmond was a friend, and the tragedy of his life was irreversible. He was part outcast, part shining star, and he was dying by the time his own sport embraced him. Even then, the embrace was confused.

"People didn't know how to react," said Petty. "I talked to him a couple of times, but when he was really sick it was hard to get through. It probably didn't end quite like it should have."

*   *   *

Before the race in Charlotte, Petty was expansive in those kinds of interviews, talking with enthusiasm about his sport—his father, his peers, perhaps his own chances in the races just ahead. Then sometimes a funny thing would happen—a wall would fall and the interview would end. Journalists occasionally grew uncomfortable. It was as if their subject had suddenly disappeared. "Kyle's a Gemini," explained Richard Bostic, meaning that Petty was given to moods and contradictions. Kim Long, the race team's secretary, said it was probably his way of dealing with a world that always seemed to want something from him.

Whatever the explanation, the wall fell suddenly before practice in Charlotte. After the longest interview of the day, Petty's concentration began to stray, and he got up abruptly and headed for the car. It was his job, after all, and at the moment it was hard to tell where they stood. The car was fast in the first rounds of practice, but not as fast as it had been in the spring. A lot of others were in the same range, and when qualifying began, Petty knew that he would need a good lap. Alan Kulwicki had set a blistering pace—179.027 mph, which blew away the old track record of 176.499. If Kulwicki won the pole, which seemed nearly certain, it would be his sixth of the year—more than anybody else on the circuit. Kulwicki was a master at qualifying. The whole thing appealed to his engineer's mind. With only one car on the track at a time, the variables were there for a man to control—the motor, the gears, the chassis setup; if you got those right, your car was fast, and you could never be the victim of other people's mistakes. A race was different. It was a struggle to survive in the middle of chaos, and no one was fully the master of that field.

Petty, however, didn't see it that way. He told one interviewer that the thing he most enjoyed about the sport was the one-on-one with other drivers on the track—those pivotal moments of drama in a race when your wit and nerve and skill were on the line, and the competition was elemental and pure. Sometimes you won, sometimes you lost, and sometimes the people in the stands never noticed. But in Petty's mind, those were the moments that a driver lived for.

Qualifying was different—one man alone with nothing to think about but his speed. Somehow for Petty it didn't quite work, and his performances tended to be more erratic. In Charlotte, for example, two weeks after his Martinsville pole, he qualified twentieth, barely making the field for the race. He was disgusted with himself as he climbed from the car and stalked back angrily in the direction of the truck. He brushed past fans who were pleading for autographs, cheerfully oblivious to his unhappy mood. Normally, Petty did his best to oblige them, but not this time. The pressure was building as they moved toward the race, and qualifying twentieth was a bad way to start.

Still, he did his best to stay calm. He agreed with Robin that the car, once again, would be good in the race. The more they practiced, the better it felt, and now everybody was eager for Sunday.

The morning came with beautiful weather, a deep blue sky with fluffy clouds and the temperature climbing into the seventies. The stands were packed, and a roar went up as the engines started at 1:05 P.M. "Be careful down there," Petty told the crew.

They got the green flag and he started poorly, losing two spots in the first four laps. His laptimes were a half-second slower than the leader's, and Rick Mast was trying to pass him outside. Then after twelve laps, things began to change. His times were faster, and now he was beginning to pass other cars—first the slow ones of Harry Gant and Derrike Cope, and then a few that seemed to be stronger: Morgan Shepherd, Lake Speed, and Rusty Wallace. He was running as fast as the leader by now, though he still wasn't happy with the feel of the car.

"This thing is pushing off the corner," he reported.

Still, the more they ran, the better it felt, and after thirty laps he was passing Dale Earnhardt to move up to twelfth. Three laps later, he made the top 10 and a television crew came rushing to the pit. They could see that Petty was making a charge. He was 8th when he pitted on lap 52, and the crew was good, changing right-side tires and adjusting the chassis in less than eleven seconds. Robin knew they were taking a risk—pitting much earlier than the rest of the field—but they could be sure this way of not running out of gas, and with fresher tires they gained ground quickly when they returned to the track. The danger, of course, was catching a caution, and all they could do was pray it didn't happen. This time, it didn't—and when the pitting finally ended on lap 65, Petty, incredibly, was leading the race.

A caution did fly on lap 69, and the timing this time could not have been better. Petty could pit for four new tires, and though it dropped him from 1st to 7th, his tires were the freshest when the race restarted. When the green flag flew, he moved up to 4th in the first six laps, and on lap 83 he passed Mark Martin to take 3rd place. One lap later, he dove past Schrader and Alan Kulwicki and was back in the lead.

For the next one hundred laps, the lead grew bigger. It was about five seconds at the halfway point, and by lap 200 Kyle had stretched it to ten. Mark Martin, however, had taken over second, and slowly, but surely he was making up ground. When a caution came out on lap 230, Petty's voice sounded almost resigned.

"How much faster is Mark?" he asked.

John Wilson gave him the news. "On clear laps, he's got you by about two-tenths."

They talked about it briefly and decided to take out a round of wedge—one turn of a wrench to loosen the chassis. But it wasn't enough, and when the race went green Petty lost the lead in less than a lap. Within three laps, he had fallen to 4th, and for the next little while his mood was snappish. "Gimme some lap times, man," he told Wilson curtly, and twenty laps later he was still unhappy. "This thing is pushing its ass off," he said.

Robin told him they would take out a spring rubber the next time they stopped, which would make it looser. In the meantime, there was nothing to do but hang in there.

"You're doing a good job," he added quietly.

Petty passed Dale Jarrett on lap 268, moving up to 3rd, but even with adjustments on the next pit stop, Martin and Kulwicki were too fast for him. He was now in a battle to hang onto 3rd, and it looked pretty grim with forty laps to go. Jimmy Spencer passed him, and Rudd was bearing down, but Petty battled back and held them off. He came in 3rd behind Martin and Kulwicki. It was a mild disappointment after leading the race, and there was a hint of mixed emotion in the pit. "This race track changes a lot," said Robin. "We adjusted the car in the right direction, but not enough before Mark took the lead."

Still, it was clear that Robin was pleased. This was their fourth top 5 in the last four races, and their sixth in the nine since Watkins Glen. They were still ranked 6th in the season's points standings, but a new realization was beginning to dawn. They actually had a shot at the championship. For several weeks now, Kyle and Mark and Kulwicki had been hot, while Elliott, Davey Allison, and Harry Gant were slipping. Mathematically, it was a six-car race, and though Kyle was clearly in the worst position—there were five other cars he would have to pass—it was a nice way to go into Rockingham, the track where he always ran the best.

Well, not always. Their last time through at the beginning of March, they finished 29th after starting from the pole. But Robin felt certain that he knew what was wrong, and he was excited this time as they unloaded the car. The Sandhills were pretty this time of year, the woods all sprinkled with red and orange, and the sky clear blue. It was the kind of day that made you feel good, and Robin was eager for the practice to start. They had put a different set of springs in the car, much stiffer than those they had used in March, and the guys felt good about the change. The car looked snazzy the first time out, moving well through the turns on an old set of tires, but as the morning wore on it was clear that some others were fast also. . . . The usual suspects, Robin concluded—Ernie Irvan, Mark Martin and Alan Kulwicki.

Kyle, he said, was holding his own, but the pressure was intense. Petty's past performance in Rockingham—three poles and two wins in the last two years—meant that expectations were high, and now, of course, there was the championship race. But this, said Robin, was why they did it. If you didn't love it now, you were in the wrong business.

They finished practice on Thursday afternoon, and got ready to qualify. Kyle was the fourth car out, which suited him fine. Best to get it over with, he said. He was joking with Kulwicki as he got in the car, trying to stay loose. It was the maddening paradox of athletics, trying to relax without losing focus, but there were times out there when you got in a zone, and for Petty it happened in Rockingham. His fastest lap around the one-mile track was 24.461 seconds—three-tenths faster than he had been in practice.

Kulwicki came next, and he was two-tenths slower, and Petty knew there was hope for a pole. Davey Allison was way off the pace, and Bill Elliott missed by more than a tenth. Mark Martin ran a lap of 24.468—a difference of $7/1000$th of a second—but Petty's time held, and one by one the others fell short. Brett Bodine and Ernie Irvan were just a little over 24.5, and everybody else was slower than that. The last car out was Dale Earnhardt, and it brought back memories of Watkins Glen, when it looked like Petty had won the pole, and Earnhardt came out of nowhere to beat him.

Not this time.

Earnhardt's lap was 24.7, and a cheer went up from the grandstand crowd. It was Petty's fourth straight pole at Rockingham, and even his rivals had to be happy for him. "Man," said Ernie Irvan with a smile, "we nearly killed ourselves trying to go that fast."

It was a characteristic moment for Irvan, who had had an up-and-down year with three wins and three poles, but too many mechanical problems and wrecks. Even at Watkins Glen, when he and Petty had the two fastest cars and the rain stopped the race with Petty in the lead, Ernie had been gracious. "Congratulations to Kyle," he said. "He earned it."

Petty appreciated Irvan for that. In Rockingham, as he had at Watkins Glen, he shook his hand and thanked him, then put on his smile and headed toward the crowd of reporters who were waiting.

Three days later, on the morning of the race, Felix Sabates was in a hospital bed. He had his own suite, the best in the place, but he had rarely felt worse. Earlier in the week, he had an emergency appendectomy, and there had been complications—an unexpected bout with fever and infection. He was still feeling rocky on Sunday morning, but he wasn't about to miss the race—not Rockingham with Kyle on the pole. He was intensely proud of his Mello Yello team, the way they'd recovered from their early bad luck—and Kyle, he said, was driving as hard as anybody in the sport. It's not that he hadn't been good before, but Felix and his wife, Carolyn Sabates, were convinced that Kyle had hit a new plateau, and they wondered if it had to do with his father. The closer they got to the King's retirement, the better Kyle seemed to drive. His remarkable runs in Martinsville and Dover, when he battled back from two or three laps down, were convincing demonstrations of his talent. More than that, they showed a level of competitiveness and heart— a *desire* that some people wondered if he had. Sabates had no doubt about it now. It was as if the shadow of the King were receding, and Kyle was free to be his own man. Or maybe it was almost the opposite of that. Maybe Kyle finally knew that the legend and the dynasty were now in his hands.

Whatever the reasons, the boy was driving his ass off lately, and Felix Sabates didn't want to miss it. He was still too sick to make it to the track, and the hospital didn't get the race on the cable. Sabates sent for a satellite dish, and settled back to watch. He had a good feeling about the day.

Even Robin, the designated worrier, was feeling pumped up as they waited for the start. "No matter what happens," he told the crew, "you guys have done a great job the last few weeks. We got a good car today. Just take it as it comes."

The engines were beginning to rumble now, and Robin glanced quickly at the faces in the pit. Jim Sutton looked tight, but Robin caught his eye and gave him a smile. "Loosen up, man. You're one of the best." A few feet away, Kim Long, the team secretary, was bouncing nervously as the first parade lap passed—Richard Petty in the lead in a place of honor, and Kyle right behind him in the Mello Yello Pontiac.

It was a good day to race, the sky clear blue and the temperature cool, and Kyle gave a wave as he passed by the pit. "You guys be careful," he said, his ritual reminder before every race.

Three minutes later, they got the green flag, and the first few laps went according to script. Kyle and Mark Martin were side by side, and Kyle took the lead coming out of turn 2. The car looked beautiful out there on the track, a blur of green and yellow and black, pulling away steadily from everybody else. By lap 15, he had a one-second lead, and it was up to six by lap 55. "Kyle is just literally driving away," declared Neil Bonnett of TNN, and that's the way it went for two hundred laps: Petty leading every mile of the race, except when he had to pit for new tires. By lap 220, he had stretched his lead to sixteen seconds, lapping all but eight other cars, and he was so far ahead at the halfway point that the television cameras were beginning to ignore him.

The tension, however, was building in the pit. It had to happen. A race was never smooth from beginning to end, but this was too familiar. Ernie Irvan had moved into second place, and he was chipping away at Petty's big lead—just as Mark Martin had done in Charlotte. In fifty laps, he cut it from sixteen seconds to ten, and by lap 290, it was down to seven. Nobody was quite sure what it meant. Was Ernie really faster, or was Kyle merely trying to conserve his car?

So far, of course, the point was moot. A seven-second lead was still enormous, with Petty on the backstretch while Ernie was entering the first set of turns. But the moment of truth was out there waiting, and it came on the 371st lap. Morgan Shepherd lost control coming out of turn 4, and the caution came out as he went sliding across the track. Just like that, Petty's lead was erased.

For everybody, the first order of business was to get new tires. Now the battleground was the pit, and this time they nailed it—a four-tire change in less than eighteen seconds. With Kyle's the first car back on the track, Robin felt good about their chances. For the last few laps before Shepherd's wreck, their lead had stabilized at seven seconds. They had also been in this situation before—big leads erased with a fast car behind them—and several times it had turned out badly. The important thing now was not to panic.

"Okay," said Robin. "Ernie is your only competition. You two are running about the same lap times. So just settle in and get your pace."

"Ten-four," said Kyle, and he sounded ready.

The green flag fell, and they hit the first turn, and Ernie went drifting high on the track. Much too high. He lost his rhythm and Kyle pulled away to a three-length lead. He continued to stretch his advantage from there, though he nearly lost it in a skirmish with Earnhardt. On lap 380, as Petty tried to pass, Earnhardt cut down low to block him, and drove him nearly to the apron of the track. Petty, annoyed, cut back sharply across the banking, forcing Earnhardt up towards the wall.

There was a puff of smoke as Petty's oil pan hit the asphalt surface. The race for Kyle could have ended right there, but the damage was minor and the car still worked, and Petty continued to build his lead. He won the race by nearly ten lengths.

If there had been any doubt after Watkins Glen, when some people whispered that he just got lucky, Rockingham erased it once and for all. This was a dominating performance. Of the 492 laps in the race, Petty had been the leader in all but eight.

"That's the best I've ever seen," Robin told him, pausing to let the words sink in. "Man, you're the best."

Some people say nothing *real* ever happens in Victory Lane, and there is some truth to that assessment. Nearly every pose is chore-ographed as the driver accepts his various awards and says nice things about the corporate sponsors. Even the race queen's kisses can be restaged if there is a photographer in the crowd who didn't get the shot. There are moments nevertheless that are uncontrived, and the emotions were flowing at Rockingham. Kyle, of course, was at the center of it all, dodging a Gatorade bath from Richard Bostic, then paying tribute to Robin and the crew. He kissed his wife, who told him she was proud and then stepped back to dab at her tears. Robin Pemberton was watching it all, standing as far from the cameras as he could. He was smiling, of course, but he seemed less giddy than simply relieved. A few feet away, John Wilson looked serene, a smile still playing at the corners of his mouth, when a reporter came up and asked how he felt.

"It's been a good weekend," John Wilson said.

CHAPTER 13

THE BITTER END

If you measure popularity by the traffic jam, racing is big in Phoenix, Arizona. On Sunday morning, November 1, there was a snarl of cars in the flat, sandy valley just west of the city, as 90,000 race fans headed for the track. (Across town, the Phoenix Cardinals of the NFL were getting ready to play for 47,000.) By the middle of the morning, the people at the race were streaming from their cars, many of them stopping at the souvenir arcades, buying t-shirts, racing cards, little plastic cars with Richard Petty's number. Country music drifted from the PA system, and out on the hill just beyond turn 4, people were spreading their picnic blankets while others were beginning to break out the beer. The Phoenix Raceway is one of the most colorful on the NASCAR circuit, in some ways typical, in other ways distinct. It's a D-shaped mile in the jagged foothills, where cactus is the most visible form of life. On the ridge to the south, every time there's a race, a line of Apaches will appear on the crest, many of them watching from the backs of horses, hazy silhouettes against the sky.

As Robin said, you wouldn't mistake it for anyplace else.

Most of the drivers looked forward to the trip. The scenery itself was worth the effort, and it was a reminder of how far their sport had come. Kyle agreed, but the track nevertheless held a measure of dread. His best finish there was 17th, and in 1990 he was 41st. With only two races left, now was not the time for those kind of numbers. Petty had jumped to 4th in the points on the strength of his win in Rockingham, and he was even more clearly a championship contender. He was less than one hundred points behind the leader, Bill Elliott, which was not a lot in NASCAR's complicated system of scoring. Under the rules, a driver got 175 points for winning a race, 170 for coming in 2nd, 165 for 3rd and so forth. In addition, there was a five-point bonus for leading a lap, and another five for leading the most.

The bottom line was that if Kyle won in Phoenix while Elliott ran badly—a scenario that was not at all farfetched—that championship was within his grasp. Leads could come and go in a hurry, and a lot of it had to do with luck—but not entirely. As Richard Bostic liked to say, you had to be good for luck to help you.

Petty *was* good in the early rounds of practice—maybe not as strong as Rusty Wallace, whose car seemed to be at the head of the class, but Robin thought they were in the top ten percent. Not that you could ever say for sure. In practice, most teams ran on older tires, and you never knew what that was doing to the speeds. But Kyle was fast from the moment they started, and the excitement was building among the crew. If they could run well here, a track that had always been a disaster, then anything was possible.

It didn't hurt that Felix was dangling a new incentive—Rolex watches for everybody on the crew if they won the championship, or even finished 2nd. It was vintage Sabates, generous, exuberant, the kind of thing that endeared him to the team. "What a guy," said Bob Romano, and you could tell by the shake of his head that he meant it.

On Friday afternoon, they qualified well. Kyle didn't win the pole, but he came in 7th, which was better than he usually did in Phoenix.

Then came the race. They had tinkered with the car a little on Saturday, and some of the things they did were wrong. Early in the practice, Robin had joked that they had enough hours to "screw up a perfectly good race car." Sure enough. On Sunday afternoon, the chassis was tight and almost from the moment they got the green flag, Petty began a fade to the rear. They hadn't done this since the first race in Richmond, but John Wilson thought they would be all right. In the course of the season, he had developed a deep respect for Robin, not only as a man, but as a mechanic. In the past, Wilson said, when they missed the setup at the start of the race, that often meant their whole day was ruined. But Robin's setups—his delicate combinations of springs and shocks and pressure in the tires—were much more forgiving. All it took was a pit stop or two, and within a few laps they were headed to the front.

In Phoenix, it happened. They finally got a caution on lap 55, and put in a spring rubber to loosen the car. They had faded to 26th by then, but now they were fast and within sixty laps they were in the top 10. The best news was, Bill Elliott was starting to have engine trouble. Smoke was billowing from under his car, and he was heading for the pits where his crew was looking grim. "Stay after it, man," exhorted Steve Knipe, and the implication was clear. Petty had a chance to win it all.

Fate is fickle, though, and changes in a hurry—and never more so than it did in Phoenix. Just before the halfway point, Kyle blew a tire. The rubber shredded on the right front wheel, and by the time he made it around to the pit, a slow and agonizing journey on the rim, he was two laps down. The rest of the race was a battle to recover, and there were times when he came tantalizingly close. He was able to run with the leaders until the end—Kulwicki, Mark Martin, and Davey Allison—but he was never quite fast enough to pass them.

"A top 5 car," grumbled Richard Bostic, "and we're two laps down."

That's the way it ended. Petty battled hard, but finished 19th, knowing that his championship hopes were gone. It was now a three-man race for the title. Bill Elliott slipped to 3rd with his engine problems, and Alan Kulwicki, the cold hard-charger whose talent and drive took a backseat to no one, was now in 2nd place.

Davey Allison won the race, and was now back to first in the season's standings. The emotion finally overtook him in Victory Lane. "It's been a real up-and-down season," he said. "It's been great, and it's been bad. There are a lot of people I wish were here . . ." —and then he wept.

In Kyle Petty's truck the emotions were simpler. It was a disappointing end to the championship dream, which Rockingham had elevated from fantasy to hope, and for a moment that same sick feeling appeared—a flash of that ache from early in the year when everything seemed to be going against them. They had fallen now to 5th in the points, but that wasn't bad if they could hold onto it. Robin was worried, but he thought they could. They were exactly one point behind Harry Gant, and only fifteen ahead of Mark Martin. With one race to go, it was going to be close.

Robin was far more afraid of Martin, who was always fast, while Gant was steady. But the task in Atlanta, the final race, was to beat either one. There was money at stake—$125,000 for 5th place in the points—but in Robin's mind there was something more important. They had had a great year—a top 5 year, charging from so far down in the points—and he wanted the final standings to confirm it.

All things considered, he felt pretty good. Atlanta had been a good track for them, and he thought they were ready for it again— if they could somehow manage to handle the distractions.

Richard Petty's last race . . .

The words sounded strange in the stock car world, historic and sad, the kind of moment you didn't want to miss, but full of unknown implications. The media had gathered from everywhere, it seemed, but it wasn't just the press. Everywhere Petty went outside the beckoning safety of his bus, he found himself surrounded by a curious entourage—reporters and corporate executives and fans, and all of them seemed to want something from him. Maybe it was an autograph or quote, or a chance to inflate a corporate ego. The demands had been building for more than a year, and Richard Petty was tired. His legendary patience was still intact, but he admitted he was ready for the year to end. That was a change. Only two weeks earlier, he had told one reporter, "I'm in no hurry.

I'll take it as it comes. For me to wish for the year to be over is kind of like wishing your life away." Now he said it was time to move on—time to be a full-time car-owner, and maybe watch his son win a championship. He said he thought Kyle was ready for that. There was no one driving any better or any harder, and drivers always peaked in their thirties. "I never doubted his ability," Richard said. "Kyle is a very talented, versatile person. He has never tried anything he couldn't do well. In high school, he decided one time he wanted to be on the chess team. We didn't even have a board, but Kyle went out and bought a couple of books, and after he had read 'em, he went down and won the tournament. Then he never played again. . . . The only question about Kyle has been his desire."

Now, however, most people agreed that the question was gone, and as Kyle made the media rounds in Atlanta—at least eight stops in the company of his father—the reason for the change seemed clear enough. His wreck in Talladega the year before had cut his season almost in half, and while he was out, he was startled to discover how much he missed it. But now, he said, as they came to the moment of Richard Petty's retirement, there was something else he was feeling as well—a responsibility even larger than his own aspirations. He said he didn't want to sound pretentious. "But next year it will be just me. The family name will rest on my shoulders."

Atlanta was a busy time for the Pettys. In addition to the string of joint interviews, Kyle was booked solid by his sponsor, Mello Yello. Atlanta was home to the corporate headquarters, and on the day before the beginning of practice, he spent the afternoon rushing from one public appearance to the next. The traffic was awful on the streets of the city, gridlocked in places, but Kyle was happy. He was talking to his friend, Jane Gossage, about disconnected topics that were bouncing through his mind—Spike Lee's new movie on Malcolm X, the beginning of the season in the NBA, and Thomas Wolfe's novella *Lost Boy*, which Kyle had added to his collection of books.

Jane couldn't help but smile as he talked. She thought the distraction was probably good for him, probably kept him from fretting about the race. She and Robin had talked about it some, and they agreed that a little diversion wouldn't hurt—but when practice began, it was time to concentrate.

The first practice came on Friday morning, and the signs of pressure were all around. Bill Elliott was sullen, refusing autographs and interviews with the press. Kyle was hyper, his attention span even shorter than usual, and Robin was angry. NASCAR had cut the practice session short—shorter at least than Robin had expected—and he still had a lot he wanted to do with the car. They were experimenting with different springs, and using lead bars to redistribute the weight. By the middle of the afternoon, it still wasn't right, and Robin was worried about qualifying poorly. A few minutes later, events proved him right. Kyle qualified 20th on a day that pointed to a strange weekend. Journeyman driver Rick Mast won the pole, the first in his ninety-three Winston Cup races, and he did it in style. He set a new record for the Atlanta Speedway, and became the first driver in the history of the track to break 180 mph. Most people on the circuit were happy for him. Mast is a popular figure around the garage, an amiable Virginian, thirty-five years old, who tells a good story, and according to one account, traded a cow for his first race car. Twenty years later, he was a footnote to history—winner of the pole in Richard Petty's last race.

On Saturday night, with qualifying over, most of the drivers and about fifty thousand fans headed into town to the Georgia Dome for the biggest Petty tribute of the year. The country-rock group, Alabama, hosted a musical testimonial to Petty, and the King was beaming when they called him to the stage, surrounded by his friends and competitors and grandchildren. "Tomorrow is the last go 'round," he said. "Nobody on earth has had more fun."

Then came Sunday and the engines rumbled, and for the last time ever, Richard Petty led his rivals around the track. The crowd was cheering—more than one hundred thousand people who had made their way through the Georgia countryside, past the thick pine woods and rolling fields just south of Atlanta, where the cattle grazed and the grass was turning brown with the first hint of frost. At the entrance to the track, the traffic was gridlocked by 7 A.M., but now, miraculously, the people were inside—most of them standing on the hard metal seats, straining to get a final look at the

King. Down in the pits, the crews from every team were on the wall, some of them cheering, while others merely stood in silent tribute. A few feet away, Pattie Petty was crying, as her father-in-law passed and Kyle broke line to ride beside him—and then it was over. The green flag fell, and the sentiment gave way to cold competition.

The pole-sitter, Rick Mast, got away quickly, trying desperately to lead a lap—something he hadn't accomplished all year. He didn't make it. Brett Bodine pulled ahead, and then, incredibly, lost control of his car. He started to spin and slid into Mast, and both cars went spinning into the wall. Suddenly, everybody was hitting the brakes, and more cars were crashing as Bodine bounced back across the track, and Hut Stricklin rammed him nearly head-on. Bodine was pulled from the car unconscious—a scary moment, but he later came to and said he was fine.

At least seven cars were damaged in the wreck, several of them badly, but Kyle was unscathed. He gained a few spots because of attrition, and continued moving up when the race restarted. By the time they stopped for the first change of tires, Petty had moved from 20th to 11th, and he was still gaining ground on the cars just ahead. "Chase it, man!" yelled Robin, but that was the moment their luck turned sour.

Kyle was one of the first to pit, and two laps later, before the leaders had followed him in, Michael Waltrip hit the wall. Robin was incensed. Waltrip was having a miserable year, mired at 24th in the points, with a car that was never in contention anymore. It was true that he had had his share of bad luck, but he had also made his share of mistakes—and whatever you wanted to call it this time, his crash put Petty a full lap down. "That Michael Waltrip . . . " Robin said, but he caught himself in mid-diatribe. The good news was, it was early in the race—not the right time for a crew chief to lose it.

Thirty laps later, Kyle was battling to get his lap back, chasing the leader, Mark Martin, when something unbelievable happened behind him. Richard Petty crashed and his car caught fire. There were screams in the stands as the King veered suddenly to infield grass, and flames billowed out from his left front wheel. They quickly engulfed the left side of the car, and the horror of the moment was almost sickening. "Oh my God," yelled one photographer. Not this. Not in Richard Petty's last race. Then as quickly as they appeared, the flames were gone. There are two kinds of fires that occur in a wreck. The worst is caused when a gas line breaks, and gas ignites from a spark on the track. In those cases, the gas pours easily from the hole in the line, and there is an endless supply of fuel for the fire. It happened to Kyle in his Martinsville wreck, when Geoff Bodine rushed through the traffic with a fire extinguisher, and managed to put it out before the whole car blew. Richard Petty was a little more lucky. The fire began when an oil cooler broke, and oil fires generally burn out quickly. The King was cool, and took no chances. He drove straight toward the fire truck stationed in the turn, and yelled for somebody to bring an extinguisher. A few seconds later the adventure was over, as Petty climbed out and waved to the crowd. "I went out in a blaze," he said. "I forgot the glory."

Kyle Petty missed the whole episode, which began as a chain reaction just behind him. Ken Schrader and Dick Trickle ran together and hit with such force that the hood from Schrader's car tore loose, and went sailing fifty feet in the air. The cars behind them began to crash, and the King caught fire when he hit Darrell Waltrip. Kyle at first was unaffected by it, but when he came back around to the scene of the wreck, he ran over a jagged piece of the wreckage and bent the metal near his right front tire. He had to pit for a thirty-second repair, and when the race restarted he had fallen to 21st.

It took 150 laps to recover, but he had battled to 10th by lap 250, still a lap down, when Ernie Irvan lost control and hit Davey Allison. Kyle was chasing the leader, Kulwicki, racing him frantically to the caution flag, when Kulwicki did something that took him by surprise. He slowed down abruptly and let Kyle pass him. "He let me have it, man," said Petty in amazement, and his voice on the radio was choked. "God dang, I appreciate that."

What Petty didn't know was that a few minutes earlier, Felix and Kulwicki had made a deal. Sabates admired Kulwicki as a driver and respected his tenacity and fierce independence. If Kyle couldn't win the championship, and it seemed clear now that it was well out of reach, Felix was hoping that Kulwicki would do it. At the same time, he wanted his own driver to finish as high in the points as he could, and he thought at the moment that their interests were the same. If Kyle was able to get his lap back, he might be able to beat Bill Elliott, who was Kulwicki's chief rival for the championship. The worse Elliott finished, the better for Kulwicki. It made good sense to Felix, and just before Allison's crash with Ernie Irvan, he hurried down to Kulwicki's pit and made his pitch to the guys on the crew. Kulwicki bought it, and Kyle was back in the thick of the race.

He was eighth, in fact, when they got the green flag, and made it to seventh with thirty laps to go. "Just take care of your stuff," said Robin. "Just ride it out." Robin sounded pleased, and for very good reason. Davey Allison was out of the race, and so was Mark Martin with engine problems, and Harry Gant was three laps down. Kyle, meanwhile, was headed at least for a top 10 finish, and maybe top 5, which would put him 4th in the season's point standings.

Suddenly, however, Petty's engine blew a valve. They discovered later that a rocker arm broke—a pin barely more than half an inch long came loose and went flying through the cylinder like shrapnel—and the damage got worse the longer it ran. Kyle first felt it on lap 300, when the motor didn't respond as Terry Labonte tried to pass. He kept losing power every time around the track, and with sixteen laps to go in the race, he stopped for gas in a cloud of smoke. The car was even slower when he returned to the track, and NASCAR officials told him to park it. Robin argued with them, trying to buy time. The mission now was to beat Harry Gant, who was two laps behind them with ten laps to go. But Gant was running at a normal speed, and Kyle was losing momentum all the time—so slow now that his car was a hazard.

Still, he refused to bring it in. He could see that he was not going to beat Harry Gant, but it was the King's last race and he didn't plan to park. And that's the way it ended, with his car barely moving and smoke still pouring from under the hood. Officially, he finished the race 16th—and 5th in the final standings for the season. Harry Gant was 4th, with Allison 3rd and Bill Elliott 2nd. Alan Kulwicki won the championship, the first of his career, and he was now the toast of the NASCAR world—a man who ran his own team and won on the strength of his tenacity and skill. Later, Kyle would be happy for him, but in the minutes of quiet right after the race, he had his own thoughts to try to sort out. He was disappointed, of course. If he had beaten Harry Gant, he would have finished at least one place higher in the points, and if his motor had held up, he would have ended the year with a top-10 finish. But there was no use crying about it now. The deadliest question in the sport was what if—and the new year was only twelve weeks away.

THE MORNING AFTER

There was not a lot of time for looking back. The guys on the crew were at work Monday morning. There were motors to build and new cars to prepare for the '93 season, and the time was always shorter than it seemed. But just before Christmas they took a break. Felix called them together for a party and told them he was proud of what they had done. To underscore the point he gave out more than $100,000 in Christmas bonuses—$9,600 each to 11 crew members who traveled every week.

Felix knew, but didn't say, that it was a drop in the bucket compared to what they had spent that season: $1.5 million for the team's payroll, $364,000 for travel, $361,000 for tires. All together, their expenses were $5.7 million—which was what it took to have a good year. Their Mello Yello sponsorship paid for part of it, and Kyle won $1.1 million, which he split with the team; but much of the difference came from

Felix, and though he didn't want to say how much, it was enough to make racing an expensive hobby. Nevertheless, it got in his blood. Felix said it had changed him for the better—made him more patient and less demanding, for racing was a world of team-work and luck, reluctant to bend to the will of one man. "It's taught me humility," he said with a smile.

For Sabates the greatest pleasure of all was the change he had seen through the years in his driver. When he first hired Kyle in 1988, there were people who advised him not to do it. The rap, of course, was that Petty was a flake, a dilettante prince who was too busy dabbling in country music, or collecting rare books, to compete with the same sense of purpose as his father. There was a measure of truth in that criticism. Kyle was happy-go-lucky and loose, which was part of his charm, but Sabates also saw other things—a lack of greed when they talked about money, a willing-ness to deal in handshakes and trust, a concern and compassion toward the people around him. "I do things with people because I like them," he said, and Kyle Petty qualified from the start.

Their first year together was rocky—only one top five in nine-teen starts, and for a man like Sabates, successful in business and generally accustomed to getting his way, it was lesson number one in the art of patience. Then 1990 brought a breakthrough win, their first in Rockingham, which carried the biggest purse in the history of NASCAR—and from that point on, Felix thought he saw a change. It was as if Kyle's sense of the possibilities was greater, his belief in his ability to make his own mark. The change continued in 1991, when Kyle got hurt and absence from the track made his heart grow fond, but '92 was the season when it all came together. Looking back from the vantage point of December, Felix thought it was mostly a question of maturity—of Kyle now knowing exactly what he wanted. But there had also been some changes in the team, and the most important of those was Robin. He was the only new-comer when the season began, but it didn't take him long to make his mark. Nobody worked harder or gave more credit to the people around him, and his greatest gift of all was dealing with Kyle. He understood instinctively that Petty's self-confidence was more than skin-deep, but so was his need for reassurance, and the chemistry that came out of that understanding was something that the Mello Yello team had never had.

It was about midyear before the ingredients came together, but from that point on, they had the best record on the Winston Cup circuit. In January of 1993, as they prepared to go to Daytona again, reporters were asking if the momentum would carry. Petty was hesitant to make any predictions. There were too many variables that were hard to control. NASCAR had changed the Pontiacs again, tinkering slightly with the dimensions of the car in an effort to improve the aerodynamics. Kyle and Robin both thought it would help, but it would take a little time to fine-tune the change. In addition to that, there had been a setback. During a week of Daytona testing, four crew members were in a wreck—a bad one— on the way to their motel. No one was killed, but the injuries were serious, and a team where turnover had never been a problem now faced a season with four substitutes.

Still, their expectations were high, and hopes for a championship were real. "Early in my career," said Kyle, "I had one bad year after another. That momentum kept carrying over. I don't know why this shouldn't be the same."

That was the feeling they brought to Daytona, the greatest race of all, where the crowds were the biggest and the infield party lasted for a week, and the adrenaline rush of anticipation was made even stronger by the need to hope.

It was the common prayer of every driver on the circuit. Maybe this year will finally be the one . . . .

All the early signs were good—so good, in fact, that it was a little bit scary. Kyle's car was the fastest in pre-race testing, and a few days later he won the Daytona pole. His expectations were soaring by now. He knew it was dangerous to hope too much, but as he began the 1993 season, there were two ambitions that defined his career. The first, of course, was to win a championship, but the second ambition was nearly as strong, and he could feel it now almost as an ache. He wanted to win the Daytona 500, to take his place beside his father, Richard Petty, and his grandfather, Lee, in the most famous winners circle in NASCAR.

When the race began, he clearly had a chance. He faded early, but rushed from 7th to 1st on lap 17, and was leading again at the halfway point when disaster suddenly struck him in the pits. On a routine stop, Scott Palmer, the substitute gas man, slipped as he was going over the wall and only managed to get the tank half full. Petty had to make an extra stop, which dropped him from 1st to 27th place, but he was beginning to battle his way through the field when there was a wreck on the frontstretch just ahead. Dale Earnhardt was the culprit this time. He clipped the right rear of Al Unser, Jr., and sent him spinning into Bobby Hillin. Hillin lost control and went sliding through the grass, and then drifted slowly back toward the track. Petty could hardly believe his eyes. Hillin had plenty of time to stop, and his wheels were locked on his slide through the grass. But now he was rolling, as if he had taken his foot off the brake, and it was almost like a slow motion nightmare— Hillin drifting lazily up the track, while Petty veered high to try to avoid him. But Hillin kept drifting and they hit with a crunch, and though neither car was traveling fast, the angle of impact crippled them both. Petty's emotions were a rollercoaster now, from rage to disbelief and back again.

"Why in God's name," he yelled toward Hillin, "did you take your foot off the fucking brake?"

Petty stalked away, but now it was Hillin's turn to be enraged. Normally, like Petty, he's an easy-going man, not given to public displays of his temper. But he later said he had no brakes, and when Petty's insult clearly hit a nerve, he jumped from his car and caught up with Kyle near the edge of the garage. There was a little bit of pushing before they separated, and it made for a dramatic piece of television. But Petty's frustration went deeper than Bobby Hillin. He made his way to his transporter truck, and put his head in his hands and for the next few minutes he was hard to console. Richard Petty tried. He rushed to the truck and told Kyle stiffly that he had to shake it off. There would be other days—other opportunities to win in Daytona.

Pattie Petty was sitting nearby, and she knew that Richard was trying to help, trying to reach out to a son in distress. But at the moment he was only making things worse, and Pattie was relieved when he finally walked away. Kyle wasn't ready to shake it off. He was caught in the magnitude of his own disappointment—his lost opportunity, as one team member put it, "to show that he was really deserving of his name." Most of the time he didn't think that way—didn't wallow in the burden of being Richard Petty's son. But on some level it was always there, and at the moment at least, he wanted to cry—and felt if he started that he might never stop.

It was then that Felix Sabates walked in. He put his arm around Kyle and said the things that a father ought to say: "Kyle, we love you. There will be other days."

They sat there quietly for the next several minutes, and after a while, as their emotions slowly calmed, Kyle already was sorting through the pieces. He was grateful for the tenderness of Felix Sabates, his freedom and ease with the range of his feelings, but he also knew that Richard Petty was right. It really was important to shake it off. They had another race in less than two weeks, and as they moved on to Rockingham and beyond, it was important to remember a hard piece of truth. Racing would drive you crazy if you let it.

Whatever its lures and irresistable rewards, it was still a sport that could break a man's heart.

KYLE PETTY'S 1992 SEASON

	Start	Finish	Points Standing	Winner
Daytona Beach, FL	33	6	6	Allison
Rockingham, NC	1	29	9	Elliott
Richmond, VA	3	20	14	Elliott
Atlanta, GA	15	8	9	Elliott
Darlington, SC	17	27	13	Elliott
Bristol, TN	23	19	15	Kulwicki
North Wilkesboro, NC	15	28	20	Allison
Martinsville, VA	17	18	21	Martin
Talladega, AL	9	10	19	Allison
Charlotte, NC	16	2	19	Allison
Charlotte, NC	2	3	13	Earnhardt
Dover, DE	16	29	16	Gant
Sonoma, CA	19	12	15	Irvan
Pocono, PA	5	6	15	Kulwicki
Brooklyn, MI	17	4	11	Allison
Daytona Beach, FL	12	14	13	Irvan
Pocono, PA	13	7	11	D. Waltrip
Talladega, AL	6	6	11	Irvan
Watkins Glen, NY	2	1	9	K. Petty
Brooklyn, MI	15	6	6	Gant
Bristol, TN	26	4	6	D. Waltrip
Darlington, SC	30	7	6	D. Waltrip
Richmond, VA	17	12	7	R. Wallace
Dover, DE	16	3	6	Rudd
Martinsville, VA	1	4	6	G. Bodine
North Wilkesboro, NC	4	3	6	G. Bodine
Charlotte, NC	20	3	6	Martin
Rockingham, NC	1	1	4	K. Petty
Phoenix, AZ	7	19	5	Allison
Atlanta, GA	20	16	5	Elliott

Wins: 2
Poles: 3
Outside Poles: 2
Top Fives: 9*
Top Tens: 17*
Final Standing in Points: 5th
Money Won: $1,107,063

*Does not count
the Winston
all-star race.

RACE NAMES AND LOCATIONS

Daytona 500 by STP	Daytona Beach, Florida
Goodwrench 500	Rockingham, North Carolina
Pontiac Excitement 400	Richmond, Virginia
Motorcraft 500	Atlanta, Georgia
Transouth 500	Darlington, South Carolina
Food City 500	Bristol, Tennessee
First Union 400	North Wilkesboro, North Carolina
Hanes 500	Martinsville, Virginia
Winston 500	Talladega, Alabama
The Winston	Charlotte, North Carolina
Coca-Cola 600	Charlotte, North Carolina
Budweiser 500	Dover, Delaware
Save Mart 300	Sonoma, California
Champion Spark Plug 500	Pocono, Pennsylvania
Miller Genuine Draft 400	Brooklyn, Michigan
Pepsi 400	Daytona Beach, Florida
Miller Genuine Draft 500	Pocono, Pennsylvania
Diehard 500	Talladega, Alabama
Bud at the Glen	Watkins Glen, New York
Champion 400	Brooklyn, Michigan
Bud 500	Bristol, Tennessee
Mountain Dew Southern 500	Darlington, South Carolina
Miller Genuine Draft 400	Richmond, Virginia
Peak Antifreeze 500	Dover, Delaware
Goody's 500	Martinsville, Virginia
Tyson Holly Farms 400	North Wilkesboro, North Carolina
Mello Yello 500	Charlotte, North Carolina
AC Delco 500	Rockingham, North Carolina
Pyroil 500	Phoenix, Arizona
Hooter's 500	Atlanta, Georgia

1992 At A Glance

Top 20 Winston Cup Points		Poles	
Alan Kulwicki	4078	Alan Kulwicki	6
Bill Elliott	4068	Sterling Marlin	5
Davey Allison	4015	**Kyle Petty**	**3**
Harry Gant	3955	Ernie Irvan	3
Kyle Petty	**3945**	Bill Elliott	2
Mark Martin	3887	Davey Allison	2
Ricky Rudd	3735	Dale Earnhardt	1
Terry Labonte	3674	Ricky Rudd	1
Darrell Waltrip	3659	Mark Martin	1
Sterling Marlin	3603	Darrell Waltrip	1
Ernie Irvan	3580	Brett Bodine	1
Dale Earnhardt	3574	Rusty Wallace	1
Rusty Wallace	3556	Ken Schrader	1
Morgan Shepherd	3549	Rick Mast	1
Brett Bodine	3491		
Geoff Bodine	3437	*Most Top-Ten Finishes*	
Ken Schrader	3404		
Ted Musgrave	3315	Ricky Rudd	18
Dale Jarrett	3251	**Kyle Petty**	**17**
Dick Trickle	3097	Alan Kulwicki	17
		Bill Elliott	17
Wins		Davey Allison	17
		Mark Martin	17
Bill Elliott	5	Terry Labonte	16
Davey Allison	5	Harry Gant	15
Ernie Irvan	3	Dale Earnhardt	15
Darrell Waltrip	3	Darrell Waltrip	13
Kyle Petty	**2**	Sterling Marlin	13
Alan Kulwicki	2	Brett Bodine	13
Harry Gant	2	Geoff Bodine	11
Mark Martin	2	Ken Schrader	11
Geoff Bodine	2	Ernie Irvan	11
Ricky Rudd	1	Morgan Shepherd	11
Dale Earnhardt	1	Dick Trickle	9
Rusty Wallace	1	Dale Jarrett	8
		Ted Musgrave	7
		Jimmy Hensley	4
		Hut Stricklin	4

197

KYLE PETTY'S CAREER RECORD

Year	Wins	2nd	3rd	4th	5th	6th–10th	Poles	Races
1992	2	0	4	3	0	8	3	29
1991	1	1	0	0	0	2	2	18
1990	1	0	0	1	0	12	2	29
1989	0	0	0	1	0	4	0	19
1988	0	0	0	0	2	6	0	29
1987	1	1	4	0	0	8	0	29
1986	1	0	1	0	2	10	0	29
1985	0	1	1	1	4	5	0	29
1984	0	0	0	0	1	5	0	30
1983	0	0	0	0	0	2	0	30
1982	0	1	0	1	0	2	0	29
1981	0	0	0	0	1	9	0	31
1980	0	0	0	0	0	6	0	15
1979	0	0	0	0	0	1	0	5
Totals	6	4	10	7	10	80	7	341

Richard Petty's Career Record

Year	Wins	2nd	3rd	4th	5th	6th–10th	Poles	Races
1992	0	0	0	0	0	0	0	29
1991	0	0	0	0	0	1	0	29
1990	0	0	0	0	0	1	0	29
1989	0	0	0	0	0	0	0	25
1988	0	0	1	0	0	4	0	29
1987	0	1	3	2	3	5	0	29
1986	0	1	2	1	0	7	0	29
1985	0	0	1	0	0	12	0	28
1984	2	0	0	2	1	8	0	30
1983	3	1	1	1	3	12	0	30
1982	0	5	2	1	1	7	0	30
1981	3	1	4	3	1	4	0	31
1980	2	4	3	2	4	3	0	31
1979	5	7	2	4	5	4	1	31
1978	0	3	3	3	2	6	0	30
1977	5	6	6	2	1	3	5	30
1976	3	9	3	4	0	3	1	30
1975	13	5	3	0	0	3	3	30
1974	10	8	4	0	0	1	7	30
1973	6	6	1	2	0	1	3	28
1972	8	9	5	2	1	2	3	31
1971	21	8	7	2	0	3	9	46
1970	19	4	0	0	2	4	9	40
1969	10	9	9	0	3	4	6	50
1968	16	6	5	2	2	2	12	49
1967	27	7	2	1	1	1	18	48
1966	8	9	3	0	0	1	15	39
1965	4	4	2	0	0	0	7	14
1964	9	14	11	0	2	5	8	61
1963	13	10	2	4	1	8	8	54
1962	8	9	8	5	2	6	4	52
1961	2	4	4	5	3	4	2	42
1960	3	7	3	3	1	13	2	40
1959	0	1	2	1	1	3	0	22
1958	0	0	0	0	0	1	0	9
Totals	200	158	102	52	40	142	123	1,156

Career Wins

*Active Drivers**		*Top 15**	
Darrell Waltrip	84	Richard Petty	200
Dale Earnhardt	53	David Pearson	105
Bill Elliott	39	Darrell Waltrip	84
Rusty Wallace	21	Bobby Allison	84
Buddy Baker	19	Cale Yarborough	83
Harry Gant	18	Lee Petty	54
Davey Allison	18	Dale Earnhardt	53
Ricky Rudd	13	Ned Jarrett	50
Geoff Bodine	13	Junior Johnson	50
Terry Labonte	10	Herb Thomas	48
A. J. Foyt	7	Buck Baker	46
Mark Martin	7	Tim Flock	40
Kyle Petty	**6**	Bill Elliott	39
Ernie Irvan	6	Bobby Isaac	37
Dave Marcis	5	Fireball Roberts	34
Alan Kulwicki	5		
Ken Schrader	4	*Totals as of the end of 1992	
Charlie Glotzbach	4		
Morgan Shepherd	3		
Derrike Cope	2		
James Hylton	2		
Bobby Hillin, Jr.	1		
Lake Speed	1		
Phil Parsons	1		
Greg Sacks	1		
Dale Jarrett	1		
Brett Bodine	1		

*Drivers who raced at least once in 1992; totals as of the end of 1992

INDEX

INDEX

INDEX

INDEX